THE
FINISH LINE

Stories of Hope Through Bible Translation

BOB CRESON
with Carol Schatz

D1417779

© 2014

Visit Wycliffe's website at www.wycliffe.org.

The Finish Line
© 2014 by Bob Creson
Published by Wycliffe Bible Translators, Inc.

Cover design by Devon Hoernschemeyer. Cover photo by Heather Pubols. All rights reserved.

ISBN 978-0-938978-25-1

Printed in the United States of America

First printing 2014 by Wycliffe Bible Translators, Inc.

D

DEDICATION

This book is dedicated to the Wycliffe Bible Translators team—staff, partners, and investors—who have sacrificed for over eighty years to overcome the injustice of Bible poverty for unreached people groups around the world.

Table of Contents

A
ACKNOWLEDGMENTS

This is really God's story, not mine. The Bible, and in particular the New Testament, is a missionary story—God's mission and the extent He will go for each man, woman, and child, giving them the opportunity to be redeemed, reconciled, and restored.

In his book *Understanding Christian Mission: Participation in Suffering and Glory,* Scott Sunquist refers to the missionary nature of the New Testament: "It is meant to be translated—to fully embody—into every language and culture. More than that, I affirm, alongside many others, that the New Testament is a missionary document."[1] The Bible is the story of God's mission. The following stories try to illustrate this point.

This book would not have been possible without Carol Schatz. Carol helped facilitate the translation of the New Testament for the Teribe people of Panama. For the past ten years, I have had the privilege of working with Carol, who has faithfully written and rewritten stories

---

1 Scott W. Sunquist, *Understanding Christian Mission: Participation in Suffering and Glory* (Grand Rapids, MI: Baker Academic, 2013), 199.

we've gathered, making me sound better than I deserve. Our family has walked this path for over thirty years with a team of people—Wycliffe staff and our support team. You "own" a piece of each story.

Finally, to my wife, Dallas, and our (now adult) children—we have walked this path together and I am grateful.

F

FOREWORD

We have been waiting for this moment for two thousand years. For the first time in Christian history, we can clearly see the finish line of the Great Commission. Never before have the numbers we use to measure "unreached" people been declining so precipitously, and never before have we been able to see the finish line as we can today. You can almost touch it, and by God's grace, we are those allowed to live during this consequential time.

Finishing the Great Commission is not only an opportunity available to us, but also an obligation. And I know no one more obsessed with this—and more equipped to usher in the end—than Bob Creson and the thousands of personnel he leads at Wycliffe.

Among my favorite memories is the time that Bob and I were once together in a remote town in the high mountains of Peru. We were there celebrating with people who were—for the first time in human history—now able to read the New Testament in their native tongue. I wept as I watched those dear people worship God with a kind of zeal I had rarely seen before.

I will never forget the moment I reached down to touch a copy of the newly translated Bible sitting on the chair of a little boy. The little boy, who dearly loved his new Bible, turned around and pointed his finger in my direction and shook it from side to side, giving me a universally recognized, "Don't touch my new Bible."

I couldn't help but imagine what God will do with this little boy who loves his Bible so much. Because of Wycliffe, and organizations like it, countless individuals now have access to Jesus' words, though they didn't just a few years ago.

Bob has written his book at a perfect time. The fields are *truly* ripe for harvest, but we need more workers. This generation has been given the resources to do something historic, and we intend to do it.

We are without excuse, and this book is our inspiration to carry God's book to the entire world.

Johnnie Moore
Senior Vice President, Liberty University
Author of *What Am I Supposed to Do with My Life?*

P

PREFACE

The year 1999 marked a turning point for me personally and for Wycliffe when we adopted Vision 2025—a vision that all unreached people groups needing Scripture would have a Bible translation program in progress by the year 2025.

Humanly speaking, this was an impossible goal. At the pace at which Bible translation was progressing, it would have been 2150 before the final translation was started. Generations would have come and gone without ever hearing that Jesus had come to offer them redemption and reconciliation. My colleagues and I agreed that this was unacceptable, and we committed to work with a renewed sense of urgency—daring to ask God if He would allow us to see the last translation started by 2025.

This commitment changed the organization, and it also set me on a path toward a very different goal in my own life. What had been conviction and obedience became a passion.

Vision 2025 did not make my view of the Bible any different. I have always considered God's Word to be the foundation of life and ministry. I remember reading a book called *Christianity Rediscovered* by Vincent Donovan, a priest who served Christ among the Masai people of Tanzania. In the book, Donovan laid out his principles for founding a church in a place where the people have never before heard the Gospel or responded to the call of Christ on their lives. I noted especially his principle that when we leave the new church (as we should), we should "leave the Bible towards the day when they can read it and use it as a living letter in their lives."[1]

Donovan's words reinforced my own convictions. The Bible is God's voice proclaiming His mission, which gives meaning to every church. Without mission there is no church. The Church is the living outreach of God to the world participating in the acts of Christ. The Church carries Christ to the world, and its presentation of Who Christ is and how we relate to Him must be based on God's Word—translated and understood.

So Vision 2025 did not begin my commitment to the Word, or to helping others gain access and engage with it, but it reenergized and changed me and the way I approached the work I believe God called me to do.

Organizationally, when we adopted Vision 2025, we identified some themes to help us move forward: We committed to working with a renewed sense of urgency, in partnerships, using creative strategies, and building and transferring capacity for sustainable Bible translation movements to local communities worldwide. We committed to working smarter instead of harder. On a personal level, I accepted these goals as my own, making a personal commitment to pursue Vision 2025 with all of my heart and strength.

---

1 Vincent J. Donovan, *Christianity Rediscovered*, Twenty-fifth Anniversary ed. (Maryknoll, NY: Orbis Books, 2003), 121.

PREFACE

God is honoring our commitments. Along with our partners, we are participating in the greatest acceleration of the pace of Bible translation ever witnessed by the Church. In light of the current pace, we know that the last translator—the translator for the last language needing Bible translation—is alive somewhere in the world today!

This book records some of my personal journey and commitment to this work. It is also an invitation to you to get involved in God's mission at a unique moment in history. You have the opportunity to join a worldwide team that is dedicated to starting and completing the last Bible translation in the whole world just a few short years from now.

If you are looking for the opportunity to engage the world and make a difference in the lives of millions of people, please read on.

S

A WORD ABOUT STATISTICS

The title of this book is *The Finish Line,* which implies an end to a race. I'm inviting you to focus with me on the end of the race to complete the Bible translation task.

Bible translation takes place within the context of the Mission of God to redeem, restore, and reconcile all of creation, ushering in His kingdom. Theologians and missiologists will debate the end point for this mission, but this book is not about the completion of the Great Commission (Matthew 24:14). Rather, it's about finishing Bible translation, which I see as integral to completing the Great Commission.

Those involved in Bible translation movements will also debate an end point. For me, the end point is when all people groups needing the Bible have access and the ability to engage with God's eternal Word in a language and form they understand best. I'm not talking about revisions of the Bible, though this will also go on, but rather about the opportunity to end Bible poverty—the lack of access to Scripture— in our lifetime. I'm talking about giving people the chance to hear the

Good News message about God's love for humankind, and His call to relationship with every man, woman, and child on earth.

Imagine a world where everybody has access to the Bible. That's achievable in the next few years. We are approaching the finish line.

When my wife, Dallas, and I started with Wycliffe in 1983, it was hard to tell where the finish line was—it was a moving target. Today, because more research has been done collecting and refining available data on Bible translation needs, we have a much better idea of where the finish line is.

Until the year 2000, continuing research led to the discovery of more and more translation needs. Then, as the twenty-first century began, something happened that we'd never seen before. The translation needs number topped out at around 3,000 and started dropping; for the first time in history, this figure was going down instead of up! Today there are more Bible translation programs underway than there are remaining people groups needing a Bible translation—we've never seen this before! There are currently almost 2,200 translation programs underway worldwide and only 1,900 translation needs. While 1,900 is still a lot, remember that this figure is dropping rapidly. At the current rate, by the year 2025, while Bible translation will not be completed in every people group, every people group will have access to some Scripture.

This book is *not* first and foremost about statistics. It is the story of God moving through the translation of His Word, reaching out to the peoples of the earth in words they can understand. Statistics are, however, woven into various chapters. As you read, allow the Spirit of God to speak to you about what role He may be calling you to play in communicating this great love story and helping us reach our goal of zero—zero unreached people groups and zero Bible translation needs. It is going to happen in your lifetime!

I
INTRODUCTION

Yaoundé, Cameroon, West Africa, 1987

My wife, Dallas, and I, along with our four children, had been in Cameroon just a few months and were experiencing lots of "firsts" as we learned about living life in our new environment. Everything was different, strange, and exciting, all at the same time.

But that excitement turned to heartbreak one evening when our activities were interrupted by an urgent knock at our door. The rattling of the screen door seemed to magnify the urgency and intensity of the knock. I remember thinking, "This can't be good news."

And it wasn't.

But I'm getting ahead of myself…

I grew up in a middle-class home in Southern California, attended a good church, married my high school sweetheart, and after graduating from college, went into business with my dad doing pipeline construction, primarily for agricultural irrigation and drainage. Dallas and I had four great kids.

We experienced seven years of plenty—business was good. Then, all at once, there was a downturn in the economy and business dried up—a year of drought. Dad and I went from the best financial year we'd ever had to the worst.

During the period of plenty, Dad had "retired" and was spending a good deal of time out of the office. Almost overnight our income fell to the point that I had to lay off most of our employees and ask Dad to come back to work. He and I both had to do things we hadn't done in a while.

Fortunately we'd not spent all of the profits we'd made from the previous year, so we had some cash reserves. Good thing, too, since almost nothing happened for nearly a year. I spent long hours in the office at my desk, waiting for the phone to ring and wondering what we would do if things didn't turn around. I remember feeling very vulnerable and uncertain about the future. I invested my time in many ways, and one was in reading Scripture.

God impressed upon me a passage from Jeremiah: "...Blessed are those who trust in the Lord and have made the Lord their hope and confidence. They are like trees planted along a riverbank, with roots that reach deep into the water. Such trees are not bothered by the heat or worried by long months of drought. Their leaves stay green, and they never stop producing fruit" (Jeremiah 17:7–8).

I clung to those verses, memorized them, and repeated them often.

During that year of drought in the business, God dealt intensely with me, and with Dallas as well, about a change He would bring about; we just didn't know what He was preparing us for at the time.

While we wondered what God was doing, He continued to provide for us (à la Jeremiah 17), but He also used the time to pry us out of our complacency. Having grown comfortable with our middle-class lifestyle, we began to examine how we would invest the next portion of our lives. The more we thought about it, the more uncomfortable we became. As Dallas puts it, "We began to feel as if we had our shoes on the wrong feet!"

As we explored these new feelings, we began to share them with a few people. One of these was our Sunday school teacher, who had been a longtime missionary to the Belgian Congo. We asked him if God could be asking us to make a move. His response was thoughtful, saying, "If it gets harder to stay than to go, that could be one indication that God is stirring your hearts and asking you to make a move."

After twelve months, business started coming back—not quite to what it was before, but back to a level that should have allowed us to become comfortable again—but we could not. We continued to feel as if we might be headed for something different, even though we didn't know what that might be. It was getting harder and harder to stay put. It seemed easier and easier to go into an uncertain future than to remain where we were.

We wondered if God might be leading us toward missions. We did some checking on possibilities, and Wycliffe Bible Translators responded with opportunities to further Bible translation that intrigued us.

Having been transformed by God's Word ourselves, we found it very attractive to think that we could be a part of helping people who had never heard one word of Scripture in their own language hear Jesus speak to them in words they could truly understand. We learned that Wycliffe exists to eradicate Bible poverty—the lack of understandable Scripture in a useable form—so that all language communities will have access to God's Word and have the opportunity to be transformed by it, ultimately reflecting God's glory. We decided we wanted to be a part of that.

As winter changed to spring, we knew we could no longer hold back. We had to open the next door, even if the future was uncertain. I'll never forget the day I told my dad that we wanted to go to a training session for new Wycliffe staff that would take place starting in June of 1983.

Waiting until Dad was leaving for the day, I asked if I could talk to him for a minute. I delivered my message quickly, doing the best I could to let him know how strongly we felt, yet not knowing, really, if we would do anything more than just go to the nine-week training session.

Dad listened quietly and then started to get tears in his eyes.

I thought, "Wow, now I've done it—I've let him down!"

But he surprised me by saying, "Your mother and I always knew this day was coming." He went on to recount the story of my dedication as a baby. The pastor, taking me in his arms, had said, "Bob and Betty, are you willing to let this little boy go wherever God calls him?" Dad said they'd replied, "Of course." Then the pastor added, "Even if that means as a missionary to Africa?"

At that point, it was simply a question, probably designed to help my parents understand what dedication of this little boy really meant, but I've come to understand it as prophetic. Even then, as I talked with my dad in the office, Africa wasn't in the forefront of our thinking, much less Cameroon.

Nevertheless, Cameroon is exactly where we found ourselves just a few years later, working with one of Wycliffe's primary partners, SIL.[1]

---

1 Founded nearly eighty years ago, SIL International is a faith-based organization that studies, documents, and assists in developing the world's lesser-known languages. SIL's staff shares a Christian commitment to service, academic excellence, and professional engagement through literacy, linguistics, translation, and other academic disciplines. SIL makes its services available to all without regard to religious belief, political ideology, gender, race, or ethnic background.

And that's where we were when we heard that disconcerting knock on the front door.

The Bolioki and Creson families shortly after our arrival in Cameroon

It turned out to be one of our Cameroonian staff hurrying to tell me that my good friend and colleague Léonard Bolioki and his son, Tonton[2], had been in a very serious accident. Both had been taken to the hospital.

A longtime staff member, Léonard managed our training center. He was also a gifted Bible teacher and Bible translator who trained other translators.

Tonton was a remarkable young boy. The same age as our son, Scott—ten years old—he spoke several languages fluently, was the joy of his parents, and was a good friend to many, including Scott.

He was also a "miracle" baby. Léonard and his wife, Marie, had gone through ten years of marriage without children when she gave

---

2 Tonton's full name was Kegnam Bolioki Romeo-Albert.

birth to this healthy and intelligent baby boy. Dallas likes to describe him as a "bright light bulb." His personality was effervescent.

That day, Léonard and Tonton had been riding home from a soccer game on a small motorcycle. They were hit from behind by a taxi as they were stopping for a soda. Both were thrown into a concrete ditch. Tonton's head injuries were severe; Léonard was also badly hurt.

I rushed to the hospital. Around midnight, with profound grief, I watched Tonton pass into the presence of God.

Léonard was lying on a stretcher in a separate room. Telling him that his son—his only son—had died was, to this day, one of the hardest things I've ever had to do. He'd had a foreshadowing, since at the moment of Tonton's death a wail went up from some of the women who were holding vigil. I have no idea how they knew, but they did. For those who have never heard this African death wail, I must tell you that it is strange, eerie, and chilling.

The following hours and days were a blur. Things do not work the same way in Africa as they do in the West. Responsibility for the burial falls largely to the family. And most Cameroonians, when they die, want their bodies returned to their home village for burial. Nothing— I mean nothing—was easy as Dallas and I tried to support the family, understand their wishes, and do as they asked as best we could.

At the end of the week, we were all in Léonard's home village for Tonton's funeral, which was conducted right in front of his house.

Léonard, still gravely injured, lay on a mat in front of the crowd. Partway through the service, he was given the opportunity to say something to those gathered. He chose to read the story of Lazarus from John 11—a story he'd translated into Yambetta, the mother tongue of his family and friends. Many in the crowd were hearing this story for the first time in the language they used every day, their heart language.

"Lazarus's sickness will not end in death," [Léonard read from the words of Christ.] "No, it happened for the glory of God so that the Son of God will receive glory from this....[He] will rise again."

"Yes," Martha said, "he will rise when everyone else rises, at the last day."

Jesus told her, "I am the resurrection and the life. Anyone who believes in Me will live, even after dying. Everyone who lives in Me and believes in Me will never ever die. Do you believe this, Martha?"

Léonard, despite his grief and injuries, read the translated Scriptures with a strong, clear voice, giving his family and friends the reassurance that Jesus is the Way, the Truth, and the Life.

Bob, Marie, Dallas, and Léonard during a recent time together in Cameroon

Prior to this, the service had been conducted in French, accompanied by much noise, commotion, and what appeared to us to be inattention.

Dallas and I really thought no one was listening. But that changed as soon as Léonard began to read the Scriptures in Yambetta.

The crowd was now riveted on every word Léonard read. You could have heard a pin drop. They listened in absolute silence, with focused attention, as Léonard read them that assurance they craved—in the language they dreamed in, loved in, and used every day. The truth came home to them: Jesus understood their deepest sadness—the loss of a little boy to unimaginable circumstances.

This was the first time Dallas and I had witnessed the power of the translated Word of God. We understood the power of the Scriptures in our language, English, and we'd studied French, but this was our first opportunity to see its impact in a language where the Scriptures had only recently been translated.

I love it when I am privileged to see or learn something important for the very first time, or to make a new discovery. In this tragic case, at the funeral for young Tonton, Jesus didn't just *speak* Yambetta; it was more powerful than that. Jesus showed Himself to be a part of their village and culture. He was one of them, and as such He understood their pain and hurt as they mourned the loss of this ten-year-old little boy. They were comforted in a way that only the Scriptures can comfort, as the Holy Spirit used this story to calm their fears and provide a context of hope.

Since then, Dallas and I have seen the remarkable impact of newly translated Scriptures—thankfully without these tragic circumstances—hundreds of times and in hundreds of communities. When the Word of God arrives, a miracle occurs. It's not the first time God has been there, but it's the first time people hear Him speak the language they love—the language in which they think and feel. It changes everything.

1

LEAVE THE BIBLE

Wycliffe, along with our partners, is committed to ending Bible poverty in this generation. Believing that people suffer an injustice when they don't have the Scriptures, we insist that all language communities, large and small, should have the opportunity to be transformed by God's Word and ultimately reflect God's glory.

Together we're on the path to finishing the last Bible translation. Our goal is zero—zero translation needs, zero unreached people groups. Imagine a world where the Good News about Jesus is known everywhere—a world where everyone can engage with Scripture in their own language and everyone knows someone who can help them become a true follower of Jesus Christ.

This is going to happen in our lifetime. The last translator for the last language is alive somewhere in the world today. While in the past this was happening incrementally, today it is happening exponentially!

At the beginning of the twenty-first century, something changed. The number of Bible translation needs topped out and began to drop, and they're dropping at a dramatic rate. We are participating in the greatest acceleration of the pace of Bible translation ever witnessed by the Church. This is the period of stewardship and responsibility to which God has called us.

Luke Elliot poses with *The Last Translator,* a painting by Hyatt Moore. The Bible in the painting is unfinished, and the translator's characteristics are indistinct. Someone in Luke's generation will be the last translator. Will it be Luke?

Matthew 24:14 says, "And the Good News about the Kingdom will be preached throughout the whole world, so that all nations will hear it; and then the end will come." The word translated as "nations" in this passage is *ethne*—people groups. All people groups from the largest to the smallest. And we are within reach of that last group!

Ronaldo Lidório, a Brazilian missionary and theologian, would paraphrase the verse something like this: The gospel of the kingdom will be proclaimed in an intelligible, comprehensible way in all the inhabited world, by means of the testimony of the life of the church, to all ethnic groups, then the end will come.[1]

---

1 Ronaldo Lidório, "A Biblical Theology of Contextualization," February 27, 2014, http://ronaldo.lidorio.com.br/eng/index2.php?option=com_content&do_pdf=1&id=41.

Luke with Papua New Guinean friends during a one-year assignment in which he learned firsthand of the need for Bible translation and experimented with the translation process.

The Back to Jerusalem movement in China is a movement of the Spirit of God to take the Good News from Beijing back to Jerusalem, where Christianity was founded. Firmly committed to Matthew 24:14, the followers of this movement recognize that they are all a part of God's plan, and that His plan includes the return of Christ. This movement has inspired me to adopt one of their concepts: hastening the return of Jesus Christ.

My intent here is not to get into debates about theology or even missiology. I'm simply pointing out that Jesus, after He was raised, told His disciples to "go," and as they were going, to make disciples.

In addition, the command to make disciples implies the need to translate the Word of God upon which their faith will be based. As the theologian Lamin Sanneh points out, Christianity was always intended to be a "translated religion." He says, "Since Jesus did not write or dictate the Gospels, his followers had little choice but to adopt a translated form of his message."[2] Faith comes from hearing—and understanding—the Good News about Christ.[3]

The vision of Wycliffe Bible Translators hasn't changed in eighty years: every man, woman, and child should have the right to hear the Good News message of the Gospel of Jesus Christ in the language and form they understand best.

According to Vincent Donovan, the priest who served Christ among the Masai, we are about more than personal salvation, although it is that. We preach *shalom*. *Shalom*, he says, "is at once peace, integrity, community, harmony, and justice."[4] This can only come through Jesus Christ. He is at the heart of it…He is the Messiah.

Most of all, Donovan says, we bring hope. This was not there before we arrived. It is "a hope imbedded in the meaning of the life and death and resurrection of Christ. It is a cleansing and humbling thought to see your whole life and work reduced to a channel of hope, and yourself merely a herald of hope, for those who do not have it."[5]

Lamin Sanneh, in a review of Donovan's book, says that only in the translated Scriptures and its enculturation can Christianity achieve its fullness. Apart from this, it is just inflated rhetoric.[6] He says, "World Christianity trails a rich diversity of real neighborhoods, of people in real life situations, expressing their faith, worship, and prayer in the idioms and forms natural to them and amidst the struggles of their daily lives."[7]

2 Lamin O. Sanneh, *Whose Religion Is Christianity? The Gospel beyond the West* (Grand Rapids, MI: W.B. Eerdmans Pub., 2003), 97.
3 "So faith comes from hearing, that is, hearing the Good News about Christ." —Romans 10:17
4 Vincent J. Donovan, *Christianity Rediscovered,* Twenty-fifth Anniversary ed. (Maryknoll, NY: Orbis Books, 2003), 121.
5 Ibid.
6 Ibid. 152.
7 Ibid. 159.

We're on our way to finishing. In the not too distant future—in our lifetime—we will, Lord willing, as a global community of followers of Christ accomplish what Jesus launched as He left for Heaven.

It's appropriate to note that we who are a part of this global community hear and understand these words about the Great Commission because we have the Bible in the language we relate to best, our heart language—the language we dream in and express love in, the language our mothers and fathers spoke to us.

I echo Vincent Donovan: My friends, above all else, leave the Bible.

God's Word in my language—what a remarkable treasure!

THE FINISH LINE

2

WORLD-CHANGING NEWS

Léonard Bolioki understood the deep impact of the translated Word long before Dallas and I arrived in Cameroon. He tells this story about a Good Friday service in his church:

> I stepped to the front of the church I attended and began to read the story of Jesus's crucifixion. Always before, this passage from John's Gospel had been read in French, but this time I was asked to read it in my own language, Yambetta.
>
> As I read, I became aware of a growing stillness; then some of the older women began to weep. At the end of the service, they rushed up to me and asked, "Where did you find this story? We have never heard anything like it before! We didn't know there was someone who loved us so much that He was willing to suffer and die like that—to be crucified on a cross to save us!"
>
> I pulled out my French New Testament and showed them the passage in the Gospel of John and said, "We listen to this Passion story every year during Holy Week." But they insisted that they'd never heard it before.

That is what motivated me to translate the Scriptures into the only language my friends and family can really understand—Yambetta!

Léonard Bolioki celebrates the New Testament translated for a neighboring people group, the Nomaande.

Jesus came into the world with the intention of moving in among us. John's Gospel says, "So the Word became human and made his home among us. He was full of unfailing love and faithfulness. And we have seen his glory, the glory of the Father's one and only Son" (John 1:10–14).

Revelation 3:20 says that Jesus is going door-to-door, knocking and speaking in a voice people can understand: "Look! I stand at the door and knock. If you hear my voice and open the door, I will come in, and we will share a meal together as friends."

"Open the door! I want to come into your lives." This is the message the people understood the day Léonard read the Yambetta Scriptures in church. It's also the message our Yambetta friends understood on what was, humanly speaking, a tragic day: the day of Tonton's funeral. Jesus not only spoke their language, but according to these passages, He also moved into their village, changing lives forever.

This experience of the Yambetta is far from unique. The transforming power of God's voice—when heard in the heart language—has been experienced repeatedly through the ages.

Chris Webb writes in his book, *The Fire of the Word*, "This ancient book has spoken into my contemporary world with startling clarity and irresistible authority….The presence of God breaks into this world and bursts with unpredictable consequences into our lives….The Bible clearly has the potential to provoke the most radical and far-reaching changes in individuals, societies and nations."[1]

And that potential is being realized in more and more locations as the pace of Bible translation picks up and more people gain access to the Word of God in a language they can understand.

This is world-changing news. Today more people have access to Scripture in the language they understand best than ever before in the history of the church. More and more people can potentially engage with the Bible—God's eternal Word that informs and transforms all of life.

At the same time, the number of people groups still waiting is dropping. Every generation before us saw the number of Bible translation needs rising as more and more people groups and languages were discovered, and more translation needs were verified. But today those numbers are dropping—and dropping rapidly. We are witnessing something that no one has ever seen before: the approach of the day when the last translation project will begin.

---

1 Chris Webb, *The Fire of the Word: Meeting God on Holy Ground* (Downers Grove, IL: Inter-Varsity Press, 2011), 30–31.

Anticipating the beginning of the very last translation program is exciting enough, but let me tell you something that is even more exciting. Lord willing, the task of translation will not only begin but also be completed in my lifetime!

I believe this has huge implications for the completion of the Great Commission. The command of Jesus was that we "go and make disciples of all the nations [*ethne* or people groups]…." (Matthew 28:19). Disciples are made from people who can hear and understand the Good News. When the last person in the last people group can engage with Scripture, the stage will be set and we will see the fulfillment of the Great Commission.

As I share this with people, it catches them off-guard. This is something most people thought of as happening in the distant future. It's not! The future is now!

Are you familiar with the term "future shock"?[2] The term was made popular by a book of the same name written by Alvin Toffler in 1970. It's a simple concept: something that was thought might happen in the distant future is happening now at an unimaginable pace. Toffler predicted that the accelerated rate of technological and social change would leave people stressed and disoriented. But I suggest that we can embrace this incredible rate of change and use it to our advantage to reach the last unreached peoples now!

We are so close to the point when every community will have access to at least some Scripture in a language they can understand. And completion of the last translation will not be far behind!

---

2 Alvin Toffler, *Future Shock* (New York: Random House, 1970).

3

LISTEN TO THIS MESSAGE

On August 21, 1986, Dallas and I were attending language school just outside Paris, France, in preparation for work in Cameroon, when news broke of a mysterious disaster. In the area around Lake Nyos, a crater lake two hundred miles northwest of Yaoundé, Cameroon, hundreds of people and livestock had died.

The cause of the disaster was a mystery for many months—at least to the scientific community. Not so for some of our Cameroonian friends. Many believe that lakes are the homes of ancestors and spirits. One of our new Cameroonian friends, Evelyne, who worked at the Cameroon embassy in Paris, told us that the event at Nyos was the result of spiritual forces at work in the area. There was no question in her mind. "These things don't just happen by chance," she said. "They are always rooted in the spirit world."

At the time, this surprised us. With our Western worldview, we were looking for a scientific explanation. But now that we better understand a commonly held Cameroonian worldview, it doesn't seem surprising at all.

Scientists eventually decided that the lake suddenly emitted a large cloud of carbon dioxide (CO_2), possibly triggered by an underwater landslide. Being heavier than air, the CO_2 rushed down two valleys, displacing the air and suffocating everything in its wake, including 1,700 people and 3,500 livestock.

While I'm quite sure the deaths were caused by CO_2, at the same time, I would not discount that there is a spiritual battle underway. What is encouraging to me is that God's role in this battle has become more obvious.

Our friends and colleagues Dave and Cindy Lux later worked in this area of Cameroon with the Nooni translation project. After that translation was completed, they helped begin a multi-language translation project known as the "Misaje cluster project" for six languages related to Nooni. A team from each language is translating Scripture for their own people, sharing skills and insights with the teams from the other languages. One of the languages included is Cung, which is spoken by people in close proximity to Lake Nyos.

When they were launching the project, Dave wrote to tell me that he'd participated in an introductory meeting with Cung leaders facilitated by a pastor named George Lang, a Cung man. As he and Pastor George approached a village called Faat together, Pastor George commented that survivors of the Lake Nyos disaster had resettled in this area. After the meeting, over a meal together, the pastor continued with his story, and it gradually dawned on Dave that Pastor George was a survivor of the disaster.

In 1986, Pastor George had been an itinerant pastor. The week of the disaster, he was assigned to go to the village of Nyos (three miles from Lake Nyos) for a short-term Bible school. He trekked to the village and held services from Monday through Wednesday. He remembers that the villagers were exceptionally attentive, and as he shared the Good News about Christ, many of them believed and put their faith in Christ. Pastor George said it was the most significant response to the Gospel that he has ever seen in all his years of ministry.

One young man, however, was inattentive and disruptive to the point that an older man finally turned to him and said, "Young man, you need to listen to this message. You don't know but that this may be your last opportunity."

Pastor George left Nyos village on Thursday morning and trekked to Su Bum, a village nine miles from the lake. That evening, after devotions with his hosts, he went to bed.

Sometime later he awoke, unable to breathe. He thought he was dying. He got up, stumbled out into the living room, and found the woman of the house sitting in a chair. He told her he was having great difficulty breathing and needed help. She just looked at him.

"Why don't you help me?" he asked. Only later did he realize that she was also affected—she was disoriented and dying. He stepped outside to get air, but it was harder to breathe outside, so, disoriented, he went back to bed feeling that he was going to die. He prayed that God would take care of him and then he lost consciousness.

He dreamed that some people came, placed him in a chair, and carried him outside into the light. Off to his right, he saw a multitude of people who were in bright light. They were rejoicing, singing, dancing. Off to his left, he saw other people who were in darkness, crying and lamenting. "I wanted to go join the people who were rejoicing," he said, "but the people carrying me wouldn't let me."

He came to in the morning still gasping for air. He got up and went into the living room, where he found three children—all dead. He saw no injuries, but they were clearly dead. Confused and ill, he stumbled outside the compound where he saw another twenty or so people lying dead on the ground.

Although he was very weak, he set out for the church to ring the bell, as people always did in times of trouble. On the way he saw dead dogs, cattle, and people. He rang the bell, but no one responded. An African village is never silent, but that morning there was total silence: no birds singing, no dogs barking, no people talking or walking on the trails. Just silence.

His story went on with many other details, but the important part was his testimony: he believes God spared his life for a purpose.

It is remarkable that this man, who personally witnessed the tragic death of so many, was also privileged to see a vision of Heaven—opened to those who died in Christ—as well as to see the pain and lamenting of those who died without Christ.

For more than twenty years after the tragedy, Pastor George continued to serve God and proclaim the Good News about Christ, always with a sense of urgency—but without the Word in his Cung language.

That began to change with the establishment of the Misaje cluster project. Along with Dave and Cindy, God is now using Pastor George as a major contributor to the Cung Bible translation. Just before Christmas 2012, Pastor George and his colleagues held in their hands the first printed Scripture portions in Cung and five related languages!

In his lifetime, Pastor George may see a more powerful manifestation of God's goodness than he has seen so far. He may see the Cung people gain access to all of God's Word in their own language and respond to Him more deeply than they have ever been able to respond before.

Working with a sense of urgency—that's what Pastor George Lang is doing. As the elderly man told the heckler just before the Lake Nyos tragedy, people need to listen to this message now. It may be their last opportunity.

It is critical that we rekindle a sense of urgency about the fact that people are passing into eternity without hearing the Good News about Jesus. The depth of our understanding of this fact will determine whether or not we share our faith with anyone, much less work cross-culturally.

Jesus's claim to be the only way to the Father is the rock in the path that many stumble over. Some people will always stumble over that claim, but it is far less likely that they will stumble if they hear His claims in their own language—if they hear Him say clearly and lovingly in the language that speaks most directly to their hearts, "I am the way, the truth, and the life. No one can come to the Father except through me" (John 14:6).

THE FINISH LINE

4

NEVER GIVE UP

Are there significant events that you remember with such clarity that you can pinpoint exactly where you were when you heard the news? I remember exactly where I was on December 26, 2004, when news reports reached me that a tsunami caused by an earthquake had devastated parts of Asia. Over the next few days, it was like progressive revelation as we heard reports and then saw photos and videos of the devastation.

The Economist, dated December 29, 2004, carried an article entitled, "The Cruel Sea." It said, "How many died will never be known. … Thousands were missing and an anthropological as well as a human disaster was feared: the utter extinction of a number of unique small tribes."[1]

The tsunami brought into stark focus a reality that is always with us: people are passing into eternity still needing to hear the Good News of Jesus Christ. While I know these matters must be left in God's hands, I also know I can do something about it. I live with this tension and it creates in me a sense of urgency.

My friends Bob and Ruth Chapman also exhibited this sense of urgency.

I remember sitting in my living room one night in January 2008 and getting a phone call that shook me to my toes. On the other end of the call was a colleague telling me that Bob and Ruth were believed to be on an Ethiopian Airline flight that had crashed just as it was taking off from Abidjan, Côte d'Ivoire.

A quick call to the field director in Abidjan confirmed that he'd dropped them off at the airport to take that flight back to their home in Nairobi.

My mind flashed back a few years to when Bob and Ruth lost their two sons, Ross and Timothy, to malaria—creating an almost unimaginable sadness in them, in their daughter, Erin, and in their friends.

Dallas and I had met Bob and Ruth years before in Norman, Oklahoma, at our first training session for our new careers with Wycliffe Bible Translators. Our memories of that time are still clear, and they certainly were clear the night I got that call: two young families, six small children between us (Timothy, their youngest, was yet to be born), all at the same string of tables in the dining hall three times a

---

1 Colombo, Delhi, and Phuket, "The Cruel Sea—Asia's Tsunami," The Economist (US), December 29, 2004, http://www.economist.com/node/3521017.

day for meals. It was more than just a training session for us; it was a time of bonding.

Bob was a pilot, and Ruth was a teacher. They'd been assigned to Cameroon where we, too, were later assigned. Ruth already spoke French, but Bob did not. Following our time together at the University of Oklahoma, they did a temporary assignment in Cameroon; then went to Neuchâtel, Switzerland, so Bob could learn French.

We overlapped with them during our language study when we lived just outside Paris, France. We visited back and forth during the overlap—we went to Switzerland to see them, and they came to visit us in Paris. Fun times.

Upon our arrival in Yaoundé, Bob and Ruth welcomed us with our first meal on Cameroonian soil. Ruth taught kindergarten for our son, Tim, and their son Timothy.

Later, when I became the field director for our Bible translation and literacy work in Cameroon and Chad, Bob flew me to remote areas where we met with our translation teams working with local churches and translators to complete New Testaments and begin literacy projects.

When Dallas and I returned to the United States to take up an assignment at Wycliffe and SIL's international headquarters, Bob succeeded me as field director. One of the last trips we made together was to N'djamena, Chad, where Bob, Ruth, Dallas, and I visited our administrative team.

After providing leadership in Cameroon, Bob was appointed as the director of all our work in Africa, so they moved to Nairobi, Kenya. Erin, their daughter, had gone home to start college.

The last time we saw Bob and Ruth was in November, two months before the plane crash, when they stayed with us in our home in Dallas, Texas. As we frequently did when we were together, we talked about their sons. Bob would imagine what Ross and Timothy would be like had they lived. It was during this visit that I caught Bob looking at our son, Tim, who was then in his sophomore year of high school.

Seeing him look the way he did at Tim, I asked Bob how he and Ruth managed to cope. As he'd often done before, Bob quoted from a passage in *The Message* Bible that had comforted them following the death of the boys:

Since God has so generously let us in on what he is doing, we're not about to throw up our hands and walk off the job just because we run into occasional hard times. …

…[We're] proclaiming Jesus Christ, the Master. All we are is messengers, errand runners from Jesus for you. It started when God said, "Light up the darkness!" and our lives filled up with light as we saw and understood God in the face of Christ, all bright and beautiful. …

We've been surrounded and battered by troubles, but we're not demoralized; we're not sure what to do, but we know that God knows what to do; we've been spiritually terrorized, but God hasn't left our side; we've been thrown down, but we haven't broken. …

[So] we're not keeping this quiet, not on your life. … What we believe is that the One who raised up the Master Jesus will just as certainly raise us up with you, alive. Every detail works to your advantage and to God's glory: more and more grace, more and more people, more and more praise!

So we're not giving up. How could we! Even though on the outside it often looks like things are falling apart on us, on the inside, where God is making new life, not a day goes by without his unfolding grace. These hard times are small potatoes compared to the coming good times, the lavish celebration prepared for us. There's far more here than meets the eye. The things we see now are here today, gone tomorrow. But the things we can't see now will last forever.

—2 Corinthians 4:1–18 (*The Message*)

It was hard, very hard—they'd lost two sons. But even though they felt battered and bruised, there was Good News. There was grace. It always showed up. So they had determined not to give up believing that the work they were called to do was of utmost importance.

Bob was still in the process of getting to know his new responsibilities as director of our work in Africa when the airplane went down, less than a year after his appointment.

In the days that followed, the sad reality began to sink in. It was true: although a few passengers survived, Bob and Ruth perished in the crash. They had no idea that just a few years after the loss of their boys, they would be reunited with them—their work on earth complete.

This made no sense to me at the time; it still doesn't today. Were it not for my faith in God's sovereignty, I would be cynical. How could it be that one family could experience so much tragedy? Two boys were already gone, and now Bob and Ruth! Erin was left alone.

Even though losing them made no sense to me, the witness of Bob and Ruth after losing their sons came back to me. While they were grieving for their boys, their testimony marked my life.

Their experience—and their response to their experience—reinforced in me the lesson that all of life is about our stewardship of what God entrusts to us; we are to invest ourselves for His honor, for His glory, and for His purposes. We are stewards of our time and our gifts.

To the frustration (sometimes) of my father-in-law, I'm not a good golfer. I wish I were, and he says I could be, but it takes time and practice. "Bob, all you have to do is play," he tells me. That's the problem—I just don't practice enough. Nevertheless, I do play. And in my mind's eye, I'm a better golfer than I really am. If I have a shot at it, I always "go for the green." In other words, I try to get as close to the hole as possible, even if there is risk involved. I hate to "lay up," taking a shorter shot just to avoid a hazard or to set up the ball for a better shot later.

Now, there are times when you have to lay up. You have to evaluate the risk and decide if this is the time to go for the green. I'm not writing to make anyone feel guilty. Lay up if you have to. Lay up if your friends or family tell you they see something you don't. If you're tired, off track, or whatever the case, it's OK to take a break.

But if you're inclined—and I think you should be—to take a risk, then take the chance; go for the green! I'm not talking golf—I'm talking about opportunities God gives you in life.

Bob and Ruth laid it all on the line. Even in the face of losing their boys, they still had hope, and they persevered. I don't think they were tempted to lay up, even though I might have been. They decided to take a full swing and see if they could reach the green.

I love how *The Message* has captured the advice of the Apostle Paul to the Ephesians in chapter 4 of that book:

Here's what I want you to do.... I want you to get out there and walk—better yet, run—on the road God called you to travel. I don't want any of you sitting around on your hands. I don't want anyone strolling off, down some path that goes nowhere. And mark that you do this with humility and discipline—not in fits and starts, but steadily, pouring yourselves out for each other in acts of love.

—Ephesians 4:1–3 (*The Message*)

My experience is that living life to its fullest always requires risk. It requires a sense of urgency. It requires steps of faith. So take that step—get out there on the road God called you to travel and don't just walk; start running!

THE FINISH LINE

5

WORDS MATTER

Nothing beats accuracy, especially when it comes to translating God's Word. But translation is a complex process; sometimes changing one little vowel makes all the difference in the world!

Translator Lee Bramlett, who worked among the Hdi people in northern Cameroon, was confident that God had left His mark on the Hdi culture somewhere. But though he searched, he could not find it. Where was the footprint of God in the history and daily life of these people? What clue had God planted to let the Hdi know who He was and how He wanted to relate to them? Where was the "redemptive analogy"—that belief or practice in their culture that could illustrate the Gospel message?

Then one night in a dream, God prompted Lee to look again at the Hdi word for love. Lee and his wife, Tammi, had learned that verbs in Hdi consistently end in one of three vowels. For almost every verb, they could find forms ending in *i, a,* and *u.* But when it came to the word for love, they could only find *i* and *a.* Why was there no word for love ending in *u*?

Lee asked the Hdi translation committee, which included the most influential leaders in the community, "Could you *dvi* your wife?" "Yes," they said. That would mean that the wife had been loved but that the love was gone.

"Could you *dva* your wife?" "Yes," they said. That kind of love depended on the wife's actions. She would be loved as long as she remained faithful and cared for her husband well.

"Could you *dvu* your wife?" Everyone laughed. "Of course not!" they said. "If you said that, you would have to keep on loving your wife no matter what she did, even if she never got you water and never made you meals. Even if she committed adultery, you would be compelled to just keep on loving her. No, we would never say *dvu*. It just doesn't exist."

Hdi translator Dangwa Pierre & Lee Bramlett.

Lee sat quietly for a while, thinking about John 3:16, and then he asked, "Could God *dvu* people?"

There was complete silence for three or four minutes; then tears started to trickle down the weathered faces of these elderly men. Finally they responded: "Do you know what this would mean? This would mean that God kept on loving us over and over, millennia after millennia, while all that time we rejected His great love. He is compelled to love us, even though we have sinned more than any people."

One simple vowel and the meaning was changed from, "I love you, based on what you do and who you are" to, "I love you, based on who I am. I love you because of Me and *not* because of you."

God had encoded the story of His unconditional love right into the Hdi language. For centuries, the little word was there—unused but available, grammatically correct and quite understandable. When the word was finally spoken, it called into question their entire belief system. If God was like that, and not a mean and scary spirit, did they need the spirits of the ancestors to intercede for them? Did they need sorcery to relate to the spirits? Many decided the answer was no, and the number of Christ-followers quickly grew from a few hundred to several thousand.

Around the world, community by community, as God's Word is translated, people are gaining access to this great love story about how God *dvu*-d us enough to sacrifice His unique Son for us, so that our relationship with Him can be restored and oriented correctly.

In Nigeria, the Mbe[1] translation team was translating the Gospel of Luke. They came to chapter 2, verse 7: "She [Mary] gave birth to her first child, a son. She wrapped him snugly in strips of cloth and laid him in a manger, because there was no lodging available for them."

The translators took time to ponder how to translate some of the words, but not "manger." They immediately used the word *ókpáng*.

---

1 Mbe is typical of many translation projects today in that it benefits from a variety of partnerships. It is facilitated by The Seed Company and is a partnership between the Ogoja Language Commission, church denominations in the area, The JESUS Film Project, Lutheran Bible Translators, the Great Commission Movement, and the Luke Partnership.

"What's an *ókpáng*?" asked their consultant, John Watters. "Tell me what it looks like." One of the translators drew a picture on the whiteboard. It was essentially a cradle hung by ropes so that the newborn could be laid in it and swung.

"Read the *Translator's Notes* again," John suggested. "What do the notes say about the manger?" (*Translator's Notes* is a series of commentaries in non-technical English that are especially helpful for Bible translators for whom English is a second language.)

The Mbe translators read the notes and saw that "manger" referred to an animal feeding trough. Even as the Mbe team read the notes, they objected. "We have always used the word *ókpáng*. We have used it for years, and that's what we should use."

John pointed out to them that it wasn't just a matter of tradition. God expects us to find the words that express the original meaning as accurately as possible. Furthermore, this word tells us something profound about God. "When He came to live among us and bring salvation to us, He came in the lowliest way possible. He did not come and sleep in a nice *ókpáng* like every Mbe mother wants for her newborn. Instead, He showed us His unbelievable humility," John told them. "So we need to find your best word for an animal feeding trough."

Suddenly the one who had argued most loudly for the traditional term offered, "We feed our animals out of an old worn-out basket that is not usable anymore, except to feed the animals. We call it *édzábrí*."

"Then try that term," said John. "Put it in your rough draft and test it with Mbe speakers."

As the Mbe people listened, they were visibly moved. Picturing the newborn baby lying in the animals' feeding basket, they recognized in a new way that Jesus was willing to do whatever it took to reach them. As an adult, He would humble Himself by washing the disciples' feet and then by dying on the cross. And this humility started right from birth, when He was born to a young peasant woman under questionable social conditions and laid in an animal feeding trough.

No word in Scripture is too unimportant to translate carefully and accurately. And no language community is too unimportant to merit the Scriptures in the language they best understand. Reflecting on his experiences with the Mbi and other people groups, John Watters says, "Translation in the heart language respects the people who speak it, and through the process, it frees them to have a relationship with God in their own words and terms."

THE FINISH LINE

6

IT STARTS WITH PRAYER

I'm pretty sure that God gives to some people the "gift" of praying. My friend Edith Hanline has this gift. If Edith says she is going to pray, there are no platitudes involved—she really does pray. And God wakes her up at times, just to pray for things. She's called to do it.

Edith and her husband, Walt, came to visit Wycliffe's headquarters in Orlando, Florida. Her first stop was at our Prayer Ministries department, where she pulled out her copy of *The Finish Line*—a Wycliffe publication with prayer requests for translation projects nearing completion. It was so heavily worn that the pages were detached from the binding!

Edith knows how to pray.

And so did a woman named Jenny. In the 1930s, while Cameron Townsend was establishing Wycliffe's work in Mexico, Jenny and her husband were planting a church among the Yazai people of Southeast Asia.

Understanding the need for Scripture in the mother tongue, they devised an alphabet and translated a catechism and the Gospel of

Mark. But just three years into their work, her husband died of typhus, and Jenny was driven away by political unrest, never to return. Her prayers, however, did not cease.

Wycliffe and SIL leaders make prayer an important part of their leadership meetings.

Jenny was thirty-seven years old when she left the Yazai village.

She was ninety-three years old, and still praying for the Yazai and other people groups every morning from breakfast to lunch, when a Wycliffe translator named Mark visited her. By then the church she'd faithfully watered with her prayers had grown to ten thousand believers. But they still did not have the Word in their mother tongue. Mark had the joy of telling her that he was working toward starting a Bible translation project. He was studying the language with three Yazai speakers while he prayed for an opportunity to meet church members interested in launching a translation project.

The next year, 1997, Mark met two brothers who were Yazai church leaders. They told him they'd been praying for four years for someone to come help them translate the Bible. "Four years?" said Mark. "I've been studying the language for four years and praying for a translation team!" The Yazai joyfully formed a translation committee, and Mark became the translation advisor who checked the material.

Individuals and whole communities threw themselves enthusiastically into the project. The lead translator was so committed that when he married, he and his bride spent their honeymoon at a training event. The future chairman of the translation committee, a paralyzed man, read in the Gospels that Jesus healed paralytics, so in faith he stood up and walked. God healed him, and he went to work leading the committee. Villages formed their own support committees. To support the translation efforts, poor villagers agreed to drop a handful of rice into a bag every day. As the bags filled up, they sewed them shut and sent them to the translation team.

The translation committee prepared books, songbooks, audio materials, and the "JESUS" film,[1] so that everyone, readers or not, could have access to the Word. The church held literacy workshops, eventually training one hundred people to serve as volunteer teachers. Each time a Scripture portion was completed, the church published it and people carried copies around in their shoulder bags, snatching moments to read them in their fields.

Even non-Christians became interested. Fifteen followers of their traditional religion attended one literacy workshop. During the week, they learned about Christ, and every one of them found their new knowledge changing the way they thought; all were baptized as followers of Christ. Entire villages of non-Christians asked for someone to come read the Scripture portions to them so they could understand who this God was. With breathtaking speed, the church grew from ten thousand to nearly forty thousand believers—a quarter of the entire population.

---

1 The goal of The JESUS Film Project, a ministry of Campus Crusade for Christ, is to help share Jesus with everyone in his or her own heart language using media tools and movement-building strategies.

In 2009 the New Testament was printed and, in spite of opposition, imported and dedicated. One well-educated woman, having read the Bible for many years in the national language, said, "Reading the Scriptures in Yazai is like finding a whole new Jesus. The national language went to my head; the Yazai goes into my heart.

Right away the Yazai set their eyes on the Old Testament. "The New Testament is like a shirt, but we need pants!" said one man. "The Old Testament is the pants. Please help us get a complete outfit so we can be fully dressed!" The main translator went on to study theology so he could translate the Yazai Old Testament and be a consultant for translations into other languages.

Jenny died in 2003, just a few days short of her one hundredth birthday—her part in the Yazai story complete. I know that, by faith, she celebrated the completion of the New Testament and the rapid expansion of the Yazai church, but I wish she could have heard what one old man said: "Now the light of God has come to the Yazai people. Now the Yazai people will grow and be blessed."

Prayer, even after all these years, is still a mystery to me—the way we speak to God, interacting with His sovereign will to shape events that He has already planned. But what isn't a mystery to me is His choice to honor His Word. And He told us to pray.

Children can pray, too.

Just ask Andy and Audrey Minch, who helped the Amanab people of Papua New Guinea translate the Scriptures into their language. After the dedication of the Amanab New Testament in 2001, the Minches moved out of the village.

Two years later, during Christmas of 2003, the Minches returned for a visit and found abundant evidence that the Word of God was impacting Amanab lives. In fact, the Amanab people were sending one of their own as a missionary to a neighboring unreached people group.

The church leaders told Andy and Audrey that they'd received a request for help from the Umeda people, who lived a day's hike away. The Umeda wanted someone to come live with them, teach them about God, and help them start a church. The Amanab church, after praying and fasting, felt God leading them to appoint a man named Simai as their missionary to the Umeda.

Simai was getting ready to go. He didn't need to take a lot because, like the rest of his people, he knew how to gather what he needed from the surrounding rainforest. He did, though, graciously accept some basic gifts, including a Bible and a lantern. While he prepared to leave, the Umeda were preparing for his arrival—building him a bush house and designating a garden area for him.

The Minches finished their visit and left, grateful to have seen what God was doing through His Word.

Several months later, in his role of overseeing translation programs in Papua New Guinea, Andy received a request from Wycliffe USA for permission to translate some stories about Papua New Guinean people groups from English into another language. The stories were part of a children's book called *From Akebu to Zapotec*[2] produced by Wycliffe USA. The little book contained colorful illustrations and brief descriptions of twenty-six unreached groups (one for each of the twenty-six letters of the alphabet) that at the time were still waiting for God's Word. The book was designed to encourage children to pray for these groups by name.

Leafing through the book, Andy discovered that one of the featured language groups was the Umeda. Up until then, he'd assumed that

---

2 June Hathersmith and Alice Roder, *From Akebu to Zapotec: A Book of Bibleless Peoples* (Orlando, FL: Wycliffe, 2002).

only a handful of people even knew that this tiny group of three hundred people existed. Suddenly he realized that thousands of children knew about them and were praying for them. And God had answered! He'd created a hunger in the Umeda to know Him and He'd created a willingness in the Amanab to stretch their meager resources and send one of their own to tell their neighbors about Him.

When Christmas time came again, the Minches made another visit to the Amanab people and also hiked out to visit the Umeda. They found Simai there, telling people about Jesus. Not content with communicating in the more widely known Tok Pisin (Pidgin) language, he was learning the Umeda language. And with the help of a young Umeda believer named Willie, he had indeed started a church.

Prayer plays a crucial role in accomplishing His purposes for the nations, and you never know who He'll call to pray. Dallas and I were in Miami for a Southeastern Assemblies of God (Hispanic) conference, and we crossed paths with Yahaira Morales.

Yahaira's eleven-year-old daughter was praying for a Bibleless people group as part of Wycliffe's Bibleless Peoples Prayer Project (BPPP)[3]. She'd been praying for this people group for six years, and she'd just received an update from BPPP informing her that their Scriptures would be completed in just three more years. The letter suggested that she might like to attend the Scripture dedication.

Yahaira said her daughter was adamant that she would be going! She was going to start saving her money right away and she expected to be at that Scripture dedication!

---

3 In 1982, Wycliffe formed the Bibleless Peoples Prayer Project (BPPP) to recruit men, women, and children to prayerfully lay the foundation for a translation program to begin in each of the world's Bibleless people groups. BPPP prayer partners receive information by e-mail about a language group and its speakers, a printable how-to-pray bookmark, and periodic e-mails to encourage them as they pray. As information becomes available, prayer partners also receive specific news about their people group.

We were enchanted with this story and delighted at the sense of ownership this young girl had taken in this translation project. She was called to pray for them when she was five, and she had been faithful.

Prayer is the root of all we do. Wycliffe staff members Dave and Linda Marcy understand that. Soon after the 1982 launch of the Bible-less Peoples Prayer Project, they volunteered to pray for a language group in need of God's Word.

Dave and Linda joined Wycliffe expecting to go overseas, but they were asked to work in the home office because that's where Dave's computer programming skills were needed. Though they were glad to serve where they could best impact Bible translation, they relished the opportunity that BPPP offered to contribute to a field project through prayer.

They were assigned to pray for the Ik people—an isolated community in northeastern Uganda. They prayed for twenty-two years, asking God to prepare this group of hunters and farmers for the Word and to prepare linguist/translators to help them get the Word. They

Amber Schrock with Ik children.

also prayed for other needs in the Ik community, including protection from hostile groups around them.

In 2005 Dave met two new Wycliffe staff members—Terrill and Amber Schrock—when they came to Orlando for orientation. They told him they were on their way to Uganda to work with a people group called the Ik. Dave realized he was looking at the answer to twenty-two years of prayer! He found out later that Terrill and Amber were two years old when he and Linda started praying.

From the day the Schrocks arrived in Uganda, they sensed God's rich blessings on them. They made friends, helped the Ik with many physical needs, and soon began helping them translate the living Word of God into their language.

In 2009 I had the privilege of visiting Terrill and Amber. It was one of those trips where you take a small plane to a remote airstrip, get into a four-wheel-drive vehicle, drive to the end of the dirt road, and get out and walk to the end of the dirt path. That's where we found the Ik…and the Schrocks!

Before my trip, I did a bit of research and came across an ethnography written by someone who lived among the Ik for a short period in the 1960s. The author depicted the Ik as facing insurmountable difficulties. He called them a community without hope!

Is any community beyond hope? Terrill and Amber certainly don't think so. Nor do the Marcys, who are still praying. They pray for Terrill and Amber and for the Ik men and women who now partner with them in translation and literacy. They also pray for Jacob, a young Ik man who began to follow Christ in 2007 and became pastor of a new church in the community—perhaps as the result of the Marcys' prayers.

The Marcys delight in praying for the Schrocks and the Ik people because prayer focuses their attention on the front lines, and because they value connecting with the generation that will finish the Bible translation task. Linda says, "Praying for a language group keeps us connected with the heart of God for the least, the last, and the lost!"

While the nature of prayer remains a mystery, it does make a difference. In 1 John 5:14-15 we read, "This is the confidence we have in approaching God: that if we ask anything according to his will, he hears us. And if we know that he hears us—whatever we ask—we know that we have what we asked of him" (NIV).

God went to incredible lengths to provide for our salvation through the sacrifice of His Son, Jesus Christ. I have no doubt that it is His will that every man, woman, and child should have the opportunity to hear the Good News about Jesus in the language they understand best, giving them the clearest opportunity to respond to His call. Believing that, I pray with confidence for the completion of the translated Scriptures for every people group still in need.

THE FINISH LINE

7

FAITH AND WORLDVIEW

From a hilltop in Lassin, Cameroon, Dave Lux, who is helping with the Misaje cluster project (see chapter 3), wrote to me, saying:

Here is how this week has been for Alfred Njinyoh, one of the Nooni New Testament translators, who is now the translation advisor/consultant-in-training for the six Misaje languages. It is Alfred, not Cindy and I, who is really overseeing the technical part of the six-language Misaje translation program.

On Monday, Alfred's little boy, Teddy, collapsed at the Lassin school and was taken to the health center where he received four IVs and is now recovering. Wednesday, his daughter, Jemimah, was in their family kitchen on the edge of Lassin and was bitten by a poisonous snake. She was rushed to Banso Baptist Hospital where she is recovering. Yesterday, Alfred called to tell us his grandmother died in Djottin on the far edge of Noni[1] land.

We pray the blood of Christ over our teammates and know God is protecting Alfred even as these calamities come upon

1 The people group is called Noni; their language is called Nooni.

him and his family. But such things do underscore the spiritual battle underway in so many places of the world where the final languages remain to be written and God's Word translated into them.

If your worldview is like mine, you know that there is an enemy that does not want men, women, and children to hear the Good News about Jesus; he'll do anything he can to steal, stall, or discredit the message and/or messengers. Dave's report reminds us of the reality of the spiritual battles being waged in countless places around the world.

The opposition increases as translators approach the end of their work. As I mentioned in chapter 6, Wycliffe Bible Translators USA publishes annually a booklet called *The Finish Line*. This popular publication highlights unique needs and struggles of Scripture translation projects that are nearing completion. We do this for one simple reason: our experience has taught us that over the last two to three years of a translation project, many more obstacles arise than in the preceding years.

While our worldview makes us aware of spiritual battles, it also helps us recognize that God is in control and the victory will be His. It's our responsibility to pray that He'll give Bible translators the courage and resolve to face the opposition that will surely come.

In my lifetime, much has been done to desensitize us to a worldview that includes God.

I am an avid fan of *60 Minutes* on CBS. If I'm not home, I'll record it and watch it at my convenience. On November 11, 2012, Morley Safer did an interview with historian David McCullough, in which they focused briefly on bridges.[2] (Hang with me now; this really is

---

2 David Browning, prod., "David McCullough's Heroes of History," in *60 Minutes,* CBS, November 11, 2012, http://www.cbsnews.com/news/david-mcculloughs-heroes-of-history/.

going somewhere!) Some of the interview took place in Paris—one of my favorite cities in the whole world.

To start the interview, Safer said:

We go with him [McCullough] to Paris, the destination back in the nineteenth century for a host of young Americans, eager to learn from what was then the most important city in the world.

France was the cradle of the modern idea of democracy. French troops were vital to America's victory in the War of Independence, and Paris led the world in science, medicine, and the arts. And as McCullough has written, the city was irresistible to the new citizens of a new nation.

McCullough added,

They came [to Paris] in droves. They were here in order to improve themselves and to go home and thereby improve their country. …

One man [Samuel Morse], having spent time here, brought home not only a stunning work of art, an American masterpiece, but the idea for the telegraph and the idea for photography.

Others would bring back new ideas in art, architecture, and medicine. In 1871 Mary Putnam became the first American woman to graduate from medical school in Paris. Artists drew inspiration from the city's magnificent Luxembourg gardens, irresistible to anyone with a passion for art.

Part of the interview took place on Le Pont des Arts (The Bridge of the Arts) where I have stood on several occasions. McCullough said, "There's something magical about this place. I think it's the bridges." I agree. There is no better view in Paris than from the center of this bridge. Looking up and down the Seine, you see so much of the ancient city, including the Louvre. Also just visible is Notre Dame; it's magical.

Standing on Le Pont des Arts, McCullough said:

This bridge figures in the story of another American in Paris: Augustus Saint-Gaudens, a street kid from New York. He was determined to be a sculptor, and scraped together the money to study here. He got by, barely, almost starving. But he got by and he studied, and he progressed rapidly.

His greatest works are part of the American landscape. [The statue of] Abraham Lincoln in Chicago. In Boston a memorial to the black soldiers who fought in the Union Army. And in New York's Central Park, the famous statue of Civil War General William Sherman.

Saint-Gaudens went on to train many of the prominent sculptors of the day. But his story almost turned out very differently. According to McCullough, Saint-Gaudens suffered from periods of depression, and while working on the Sherman sculpture in Paris, he had a recurrence of his depression that became unbearable. McCullough said,

It was very early in the morning, still not quite light. And what he was going to do was kill himself by jumping off this bridge. …The Pont des Arts. …And as he got out here…the sun began to rise, and the whole facade of the Louvre was lit up, all the bridges. And he said to himself, "I don't want to die. I want to live." And he started whistling, and walked back up to the studio happy as can be. It was Paris. Paris saved his life, literally saved his life.

Really? Can a city save someone's life? I don't think so. I have to disagree with McCullough on this point. Paris was just the backdrop;

it was the canvas God used to display something beautiful. I have no idea whether Saint-Gaudens viewed the incident this way or not, but I believe that God was at work. The enemy intended to rob him, but creation and its beauty—a gift from God—saved him.

How we interpret a story like this depends a great deal upon our worldview. Did Saint-Gaudens's worldview keep his mind open to the things of God? I don't know, but I believe that it is always God's intent to speak into our lives through our emotional response to things that inspire us. He designed the world around us, even the beauty of Paris, to point us in His direction.

Steve Sheldon and his wife, Linda, used to work as linguists and translators in Brazil. Steve tells the story of hunting with the men in the village where he lived. While out on one of their expeditions, he asked one of the hunters how they could see so many things in the forest. Typically he never saw what they were hunting until after they'd killed it.

The hunter replied:

Steve, your problem is that the things you see are very small [meaning few]. Even with an extra set of eyes [glasses], you don't see what's important. You don't see well because you only try to see with your eyes. We, on the other hand, have very large vision [meaning they see many things]. We see things you don't.

For example, we see the colorful macaw parrot with our eyes. Wild pigs and monkeys we see with our ears [they make noise]. The anteater we see with our noses [they smell]. Snakes we see with our skin, because they make us tingle when we sense they're near. And the sky, stars, sun, and moon, which reflect the passage of time, we see from the inside out, and all over.

How true! Scriptures confirm that invisible things can be seen. Romans 1:20 says, "...Ever since the world was created, people have seen the earth and sky. Through everything God made, they can clearly see his invisible qualities—his eternal power and divine nature...."

In *Christianity Rediscovered* Vincent Donovan tells the story of a village elder who took exception to the word Donovan's translator had chosen for "faith," saying it was not very satisfactory in Masai. The word simply meant to agree to something. The elder said that to believe like that was to be like the hunter who shot a lion with a gun. Only his finger and eyes participated in the hunt.

But real faith, he said, is more like the lion on a hunt for his prey: every part of his being participates—eyes, nose, and legs. When the lion kills his prey and eats it, he brings it into himself and it becomes a part of who he is. That is what true faith is like: it fills every part of a person's being.[3]

Faith, then, controls the way we see things. The community of faith in Christ sees certain things as true and wise, even though they look foolish to those without faith. We sometimes forget that it is God, through His Holy Spirit—the gift given to us as a guarantee of our salvation—Who leads us to the truth. Without the Holy Spirit, our worldview is askew.

Keith Beavon and his wife, Mary, have dedicated themselves to making the Scriptures available through Bible translation to the peoples living in the far east of Cameroon—not an easy place to live and work. The worldview of these people does not naturally lead them toward the God of Heaven and Earth.

Keith wrote recently, saying, "Bible translation is about creating a new view of God—why He created the world, why He created human-kind, and the extent to which He will go for a relationship with us."

---

3 Vincent J. Donovan, *Christianity Rediscovered,* Twenty-fifth Anniversary ed. (Maryknoll, NY: Orbis Books, 2003), 48.

Access to God's Word, then, is foundational. As people engage with it in the language in which they think and feel, God often uses it to open their hearts and minds to His purposes. It rewrites the road map of their lives.

Pugong was a Filipino man who thought he knew what his life purpose was—until God changed his worldview. He was the foremost priest in the traditional religion of his Central Ifugao village. He understood the power of the spirits. The area where he lived was renowned for its allegiance to spirit worship, and when Scripture translation began there in the 1960s, he witnessed intense spiritual warfare.

But over time Pugong also came to understand the power of Christ. He saw his nine children and many of his neighbors become believers, especially after the New Testament was published in 1980, and he experienced God's patient love for many years. His children never gave up on him; nor did the church; nor did his Wycliffe friend, Anne West. In fact, he remembers Anne from years back as the neighbor who would not sleep at night until she knew he was safely home from performing his priestly duties, which included drinking large quantities of a traditional fermented brew.

"Yes, I'm going to accept Christ," Pugong said for many years, "but not yet. I'm still afraid of what the spirits will do to me."

Finally, Pugong found the courage to commit his fears to Christ. When a church choir came to his home to sing for him, he announced, "I'm ready to accept Christ."

"Oh, wait until a pastor comes!" they said.

"No, I don't need a pastor. I can pray now." And he did.

Four months later, squatting in a low drum of water, Pugong was baptized, and his altar, rice god, and other religious paraphernalia were all burned. At his invitation, his fellow priests were present. "I truly have become a follower of Christ," he told them, "and you must do the same."

Pugong burning his religious paraphernalia.

"It was a grand day," wrote Anne.

The Scriptures change the way people think about God; it changes their worldview; it rewrites their road map so that it leads directly to the Father via the Son. And it results in changed lives for people like Pugong.

It's never easy to rewrite the roadmap we've decided to follow, but through the power of God it is possible. As long as we are alive, it's never too late for us or for someone who has followed pagan gods to turn to the one true God. But to do that, we have to be able to understand what He is saying to us. We have to understand His Word.

8

FAITHFUL AND FOCUSED

When Dallas and I looked for an assignment with Wycliffe outside the United States, we went to our international leadership for advice. The consensus was that we should go to Cameroon.

Dallas likes to say that our response was something like, "Great! Where is Cameroon?" It was almost that bad! We really had no idea.

Well, we did figure out where Cameroon was, and we went there. When we arrived with our four children, we'd just completed French study, so we had some language ability. Both French and English are official languages in Cameroon, so we were able to communicate. We'd also made some Cameroonian friends in France, so while many things were new, cross-cultural issues were not as intimidating as they could have been.

We spent the first three months becoming oriented to Africa. We had new health issues to deal with (like malaria), new friends to make, and new ways to view relationships. We were moving from a culture where productivity was valued for productivity's sake to one where relationships were paramount and where the relationships themselves produced results.

It was during these initial days that I was reminded of the importance of pacing ourselves so that we could go the distance. After orientation our kids started school. The American School of Yaoundé was an excellent environment for their early education, and they thrived.

One of my early experiences associated with the school was climbing Mount Cameroon with my daughter, Emily. Before you minimize this accomplishment, you should know that Mount Cameroon, an active volcanic peak, is the highest peak in West Africa. It's taller than Mount Hood in Oregon and just short of the height of Mount Rainer in Washington. Seen from the ocean, Mount Cameroon is imposing. It rises from the coast to over thirteen thousand feet!

I'd seen pictures of this annual event—a challenge undertaken each year by the ninth-grade class. John, another father who had participated in the event with his daughter, Rachel, described the challenges to me. Then, weeks before we climbed, the teacher in charge of the field trip warned us to prepare. We would need the right clothes, shoes, plenty of water, etc., and we would need to train physically. We were told that the best way to prepare was to climb stairs—lots of them!

Check, check, check … double check; I took it seriously.

Well, nothing prepared me for the climb. I remember thinking, "I'm going to die on this mountain!" And several times I wished I could die, or at least quit!

At around ten thousand feet, Emily got altitude sickness. For about an hour, she was lethargic, and we moved slowly up the mountain, stopping frequently to let her acclimate. At this point I thought maybe I could use her as an excuse to quit, but she recovered and left me in the dust!

I was exhausted both physically and mentally. I'm not sure it was just the lack of oxygen, although that certainly cannot be discounted. It was more likely the lack of mental preparation that weighed me down.

This climb is a two-day event for most people, so we spent a night on the mountain, sleeping at the last of three huts climbers use to rest and recover before going on. Hut 3 is just short of the summit. The goal is to get up early and, in the dark, make the climb to the summit to watch the sun rise.

It was a very long night. Even in my sleeping bag, I nearly froze to death! We were close to the equator, but at twelve thousand feet, when the wind blows, it's cold. I had not thought to bring gloves—an extra pair of socks would have to do to shield my hands. I had brought the right layers, but things were sweat-soaked from the day's climb. I was wet and miserable.

And my shoes were not right. I'd brought my hiking boots, but they were just wrong—too rigid for the volcanic rocks we climbed.

I remember thinking on the way up, "We're never going to reach the summit." We'd climb over a ridge, I'd look up, and there would be another long ascent to the next ridge.

Our Cameroonian guides kept encouraging us, saying, "You're almost there!"

Really? Wait, there's another ridge to climb!

Morning came and I did make it to the top. I was so relieved—I made it! The climb down, I thought, should be easier.

How wrong I was! The descent proved to be harder than the climb up. My growing suspicion about wearing the wrong shoes proved correct. My toes jammed into the hard toes of the boots and my feet were killing me.

Two things kept me going: my desire not to fail (I did not want to disappoint or embarrass my daughter) and my cheering section (my faithful Cameroonian porter and guide).

I think I already knew the lesson, but it was reinforced by this experience: little things make a big difference over time; pace yourself for the long haul, and stick with it.

Steve VanRooy, a friend and colleague, once told me a story from his experience in Sudan that illustrates this.

Jalal[1] is a member of the Tennet people group in South Sudan. As a teenager, he wanted an education, but he couldn't get one because of the civil war. So he found his way to Khartoum—about a thousand miles north of his home—still seeking an education. In Khartoum he lived with other members of the Tennet community, but he barely scraped by. Through no fault of his own, the opportunity he dreamed of—getting an education—passed him by.

After several years of living in Khartoum, he heard that a translation program to translate the Scripture into Tennet was about to start. He also heard that those responsible for the Bible translation program were identifying people they thought might be qualified to work as translators. To kick things off, they were offering an introductory course on translation principles in Arua, a city in Uganda many miles to the south.

Jalal and a friend—another Tennet man—decided they wanted to attend this workshop. Jalal in particular felt that God was calling him to this task. But the men had a problem: While they believed they should go to Uganda, they had no money for plane tickets.

---

1 A substitute for his real name.

So they started walking. Though Uganda is pretty much straight south of Khartoum, they could not walk through the war zone, so they took a jog to the east to Ethiopia and then turned south toward Uganda. They may have walked all the way, or they may have hopped a bus as far as the border—the details are sketchy. But it doesn't really matter. What matters is that they believed that God would make a way, because He was calling them.

It would have been nearly a thousand miles south through Ethiopia, Kenya, and on to Uganda. They had no SUV, no hiking boots, no camping gear, and no money. None. They walked by faith—and lived on hospitality they found along the way.

It took them eight months. It was an incredible journey!

Jalal completed the introductory course in translation principles and went on to become a member of the Tennet translation team. He proved to be a natural and gifted translator and, for extra measure, an accomplished musician.

And his traveling companion? He didn't join the translation team, but I have to admit I'm intrigued by the "support" role God gave him. He stuck with Jalal for a thousand miles. I don't know his name, but I wonder if Jalal would have made it without him. I wonder what would have happened if he'd said, "No, I won't go with you." But he didn't. He said yes, and he stuck it out for the long haul, hiking right along beside Jalal.

Sebastian was another person who committed himself to a task and kept at it, even when it was difficult. A resident of a rural area in Mexico, he was fifty years old, and an alcoholic with a second-grade education, when he trusted Christ as his Savior. He began translating the Scriptures into his Tezoatlan Mixtec language when he was fifty-five—quite elderly for his small Mexican community. He had no training, no help, not even an alphabet beyond the Spanish one he'd learned in school—but he saw a need: While he himself could understand a fair amount of what he read in his Spanish Bible, his wife could not, nor could many others who attended the Bible study in their village. His heart burned to help them.

Finally one day he decided he had to try. He bought a notebook and set out to translate the resurrection story in Luke 24. It was hard to spell Mixtec words using only Spanish letters. It was even harder to understand the biblical concepts and express them in his language. It made his usual work plowing rocky fields and hauling firewood down mountain trails seem easy.

Nevertheless he kept at it.

He took his beloved notebook to every Bible study, but he didn't read from it out of fear that he might have mistranslated the precious Word of God.

Then one night as he watched his neighbors sleeping, wiggling, or whispering to each other through an unintelligible service, he knew he couldn't wait any longer. He slowly stood up and moved to a position underneath the only light bulb in the room. With trembling hands, he opened his notebook, took a deep breath, and began to read. Slowly, haltingly at first, he read those words from Scripture, gaining strength and confidence as he read on.

Several people gasped as they realized that he was reading in Mixtec, their heart language. Then the room grew quiet. No one moved or spoke or slept. Tears rolled down a few cheeks. The light of understanding shone in their eyes. Sebastian read on for a long time, and when he stopped, he knew that no one present would ever be the same again.

Time passed and Sebastian's notebook filled up. His farming suffered, as did his weaving of palm fronds into baskets and hats for extra income. Money grew tighter, but God always provided for his needs. He kept translating, and he kept on sharing those newly translated verses with his wife and neighbors. He read at four or five services each week, and the walls began to come down. God was no longer a "foreigner." God spoke Mixtec, and the words went straight to Mixtec hearts.

Sebastian worshipping with his neighbors.

Four years after Sebastian began translating, a Wycliffe translator, John Williams, came to Sebastian's village, looking for someone willing to move six hours away and teach John his language so they could make books and translate the Scriptures. John could only stay in the village one night, but God led him straight to Sebastian, who asked just one question: "Do you want to leave tonight or in the morning?"

As Sebastian and John worked together, Sebastian eagerly appropriated the new alphabet symbols that made his language easier to write. He just as eagerly contributed to every aspect of their translation and literacy work. Thirteen years later, with joy and thankfulness, Sebastian held in his hands a draft of the whole New Testament in Tezoatlan Mixtec.

Not long after that, God took Sebastian home, his task completed. The New Testament was joyfully dedicated in 2008 and is now being used by Sebastian's people in both written and oral forms.

If you or I had been choosing a mother tongue translator for the Mixtecs, we might have overlooked Sebastian. He was too old, we might have said, and his health was compromised by his former addiction to alcohol. He had neither a good education nor a very good knowledge of Spanish. He didn't know how to develop an alphabet for a language that had never been written, and certainly he couldn't translate without one!

But God knew better. He changed Sebastian's life first, and then He gave him the vision, endurance, and ability he needed to translate many chapters of the Bible for his neighbors, providing for his physical needs along the way.

Often what God calls us to do is to show up and be faithful over our period of stewardship—however long that is. Our stewardship can be marked by brevity, seeming insignificance, or what we view as small. Other times things start small and grow into a movement.

Francisco Díaz illustrates this, and he's one of my "heroes." Francisco was a young Cakchiquel believer who worked with Cameron Townsend, the founder of Wycliffe Bible Translators, when Townsend first went to Central America to distribute Spanish Bibles and tracts.

When he met Townsend in late 1917, Francisco had been a Christian for only a few months, but he willingly spent a year with Townsend traveling with him through four Central American countries sharing the Good News.

It was Francisco who sparked Townsend's vision for Bible translation. Hugh Steven, Wycliffe author and historian, says:

> One night, camped out on a cold mountain ridge in Guatemala, a young twenty-two-year-old Cameron Townsend sensed a call by God that would change the entire direction of his life. With Cam on that ridge was his Cakchiquel colporteur com-

panion and friend, Francisco Díaz. As the two men shared a simple meal of dried tortillas and a hard-boiled egg washed down with tepid water, Francisco shared (as he had done on several occasions before) his long-held dream for the Cakchiquels to have the Scriptures in the language of his birth. Francisco shared with Townsend his puzzlement over why the Scriptures they were selling were only available in Spanish. Surely, he wondered, God could speak His Word to the Cakchiquels just as He had done to Spanish-speaking people.[2]

Townsend took the challenge, and a vision was born.

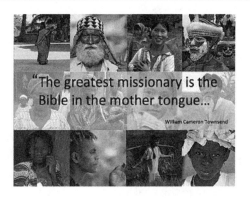

A few months later, Francisco died of malaria at the age of thirty-six. He'd been a Christian only a year and a half and Townsend's co-worker for only a year, but without question, he was faithful to his call: He was the instrument God used to persuade Townsend to switch from Spanish to Cakchiquel, from distributing an existing translation to translating a new one. The eventual result was the organization we call Wycliffe Bible Translators and the acceleration of a huge worldwide Bible translation movement that predated Townsend but was energized by God in a whole new way.

2 Hugh Steven, *Yours to Finish the Task: The Memoirs of W. Cameron Townsend, Part Four: 1947–1982* (Orlando, FL: Wycliffe, 2004), 252.

Francisco was a faithful steward, and his contribution to building the kingdom, though brief, was huge.

Cameron Townsend's own faithfulness to his vision is legendary. It never flagged, even on his deathbed. The day before he died in 1982, he was visited by Bernie May, a past president of Wycliffe. Bernie reports Townsend as saying, "I guess I'm not going to see it."

"See what?" asked Bernie.

"See the last language started."

Bernie says, "But I believe he did see it—by faith—on that mountainside in Guatemala with Francisco Díaz."

Townsend kept his eye on the prize for almost sixty-five years, and he passed on to us that deep commitment to see the last people group reached, the last Bible translation started and finished.

Now it's our period of stewardship. We don't know how long we have, but we're here, and we need to be faithful. As we think about the final push toward the last languages needing translation, we need to remain as focused on the goal and as available to God as Cameron Townsend and Francisco Díaz were.

We are the inheritors of a huge vision…and it's not just about Bible translation; it's about a love story. It's the story of Luke 15—God's willingness to go to great lengths to reach the least, the last, and the lost with the Good News about Jesus Christ. Like Cameron Townsend and Francisco Díaz, we believe that sharing the Good News is done most effectively through the language that speaks to the heart, most often the mother tongue; we are compelled to pursue their vision of God's Word being understandable to all!

9

CHANGED LIVES

I am often asked what difference it makes if people have the Bible.

First of all, it's a matter of justice. I have always felt it is an injustice for people *not* to have access to Scripture. They have a right to hear and/or read the Good News about Jesus in the language they relate to best, most often the language of their birth—their mother tongue.

Once they have access and opportunity to engage with the Scriptures, the question is, will they exercise their opportunity? That's when lives can begin to change.

Marti Giger worked in Northern Cameroon among the Daba. During her early days living in a Daba village, children would often pause and look in the windows, and she would sometimes feel like chasing them away.

Kadri, a nine-year-old boy, was one of these children. He was always hanging around her house after school, and he and his friend often stayed on and on into the evening. Marti said, "My colleague,

Ruth, and I never felt the freedom to send them away. Sometimes we gave them toys to play with, or I told them a Bible story."

Marti cannot remember how long it went on like this, but suddenly Kadri stopped coming around. Marti speculates that most likely his parents, who were of another predominant religion, told him not to visit them anymore.

Years passed and Marti moved to the city of Maroua where, surprisingly, one day she met Kadri. He was a taxi driver. He had become affiliated with the religion of his parents and married a woman with the same religious persuasion. Marti was very pleased to see him.

On one of Marti's trips to the village, Kadri accompanied her because his father had died. Later, on the way back to Maroua, Marti said to him, "Kadri, now you are grown up, and your father has died. Don't you want to believe in Jesus now? You are free to do it."

Kadri said, "I will come back to this," and went home.

To Marti's delight, one day Kadri did put his faith in Christ, or as his people say, he "put his head on Jesus." He was very eager to learn all about Jesus Christ, so Marti started weekly Bible studies for him using the Daba New Testament. Each time he met with Marti, they prayed for his wife, Fadimatou, that she, too, would "put her head on Jesus."

Kadri was baptized and renamed Moïse, all the while facing a lot of family pressure. His wife and his brothers tried everything they could to get him to give up his new faith. They offered him money, a television, even a car. Fadimatou cut his Daba New Testament with a razor blade. She poured kerosene on his clothes, intending to burn them. She left him several times and went to live with her family, but Moïse stood firm in his faith. He took her back each time, while he and Marti continued to pray for her.

Fadimatou, Moïse, and their children, with Marti Giger.

Marti says, "I'm sorry to say that I doubted that Fadimatou would ever turn to Christ, but I, along with my friends, continued to pray... for ten years!"

In January 2006 it finally happened! Fadimatou accepted Christ and was completely transformed! She became involved in church activities and began using her many gifts in the context of the church. She also became eager to learn to read the Scriptures. She and Moïse, along with their two children, became a very happy family, in spite of continued strong opposition within the family system to their Christian faith.

Marti says, "Looking back, I am sure that God had already started His work in Moïse's heart when he was hanging around our house, watching us and listening to me read him Bible stories. God had a plan, and I was part of it, even though I wasn't aware of it at the time."

The Word of God, translated into his own language and lived out in the life of his friend Marti, impacted his heart and changed his life. This happens in community after community as people gain access to God's Word and then engage with it.

Watching other people interact with the translated Word sometimes changes us as well. I've already told you how it's impacted me. It has also impacted Mart Green,[1] CEO of a chain of Christian and educational supply stores called Mardel.

During a 1998 trip to Guatemala, Mart attended the dedication of the New Testament for the Eastern Jacaltec community. There he watched Gaspar, one of the Eastern Jacaltec translators, weep uncontrollably at receiving his own copy of the New Testament.

Although Mart's work and home revolved around Bibles and other Christian books, he had never seen anyone walk out of one of his stores overwhelmed and weeping at receiving a copy of God's Word. It affected him deeply. That night in a tiny hotel room in a remote village he prayed and promised God that he would not start another day of his life without first reading His Word.

Already a committed Christian, Mart's worldview and Christian walk were forever changed as he fully realized the value of the Bible and how precious it is in a person's heart language. His life motto became, "This Book is Alive!"

In 2003 Mart formed a production company, Every Tribe Entertainment. The company was designed to make feature films about the power of God's Word and to engage the culture in the United States through film. His first film, *End of the Spear,* tells a story that took place in 1956, when five young missionaries were brutally killed on a remote river beach in the Ecuadorian jungle—speared to death by people with whom they'd come to share the Gospel.

---

1 Mart Green began his retail career with his parents in the Hobby Lobby arts and crafts stores. Today, he is a member of the Hobby Lobby board of directors and CEO of Mardel Christian and Educational Supply. Mardel donates 10 percent of its net profits to help provide Bibles to the world, including printing Scripture translated by Wycliffe.

The highlight of the film is the miraculous reconciliation and transformation that followed, demonstrating the power of God's Word in the Waodani language. Mart said:

My favorite verse is from 2 Corinthians, chapter three, from *The Message* translation. It talks about our lives as a testimony: "Your very lives are a letter that anyone can read by just looking at you. Christ himself wrote it—not with ink, but with God's living Spirit; not chiseled into stone, but carved into human lives—and we publish it."

The Waodani were known for their violence, but their lives were changed because of God's Word. He made them into a culture of peace and even enabled one of the killers to reconcile with some family members of the missionaries they had killed. That is the power of His Word in people's lives.

Once a violent people, the Waodani are now ambassadors of reconciliation—all because of the arrival of God's Book. No one has to ask if they know God—it's written all over their lives.[2]

The Bible's message of reconciliation is impacting people in other places, too. On a trip into an isolated mountain area of South Asia, my wife, Dallas, and I met a lady who is one hundred years old. Some years ago the Good News reached her village and she became one of the first believers. God's Word did not exist in her language, so she and others in her village worshipped in the state language.

She is part of a people group that has been estranged from a neighboring group for nearly one hundred years—her entire life! Their languages are very closely related, and they share a common oral history, but for the last century they have also shared a strong desire to avoid each other. At times they have viewed each other with outright hostility.

---

2 "This Book Is Alive!" *FrontLines*, Winter 2008, 1–2.

Recently, however, that hostility has begun to melt as the result of Bible translation. A team from each of these languages joined a multi-language Bible translation project—a "cluster project"—and began to translate the Gospel of Mark. Each team translated for their own people, sharing skills and insights with teams from other related languages.

For most of her one hundred years of life, this woman's people group has been estranged from their neighboring group. That is changing as a result of Bible translation.

When the teams from the two antagonistic groups finished the Gospel of Mark, they decided to hold a joint celebration to dedicate the Scriptures. The Scriptures brought the two communities together for a time of rejoicing around the recently translated Good News. According to the South Asian partner who accompanied us, this may have been the first time in forty years that the groups came together for anything. Amazing!

The Apostle Paul wrote about a similar reconciliation in Ephesians 2:16: "Together as one body, Christ reconciled both groups [Jews and Gentiles] to God by means of his death on the cross, and our hostility toward each other was put to death."

CHANGED LIVES

The Spirit of God is at work in communities with the Scriptures, drawing men, women and children to Himself with the good news that they can be reconciled to God and to each other through the message of reconciliation.

THE FINISH LINE

10

FOUNDATIONS OF THE CHURCH

It's a mystery, at least to me, that Jesus would choose things that are powerless to shame the powerful, and things the world considers foolish to shame the wise. It's also a mystery that He uses people to build His kingdom here on earth and to establish His people, the Church. It seems counterintuitive to me, but that was His choice—mainly, I'm sure, so none of us could take credit for it or boast.

Steve Payne, one of my colleagues who worked in Senegal, once wrote me saying:

We went to Senegal in 1990. We were expecting that we would be assigned to a large language group, one with hundreds of thousands or perhaps even a million speakers. But when we arrived, we found that all the larger languages already had translators assigned to them.

The top three priorities for unreached people needing Bible translation that we were asked to consider and pray about all had less than ten thousand speakers.

Of those three, God seemed to be clearly leading us to work with the Kwatay, a group of only about five thousand people. I remember walking through the main Kwatay village the night we visited there. I stopped to watch a full moon rise over the point of a grass-roofed hut.

A voice seemed to come to me: "Is it really worth giving your whole life to bringing God's Word to just five thousand people?" I struggled with that. It wasn't as obvious to me that night as it is now, where that voice was coming from.

But then it was as if I heard another voice. It said, "How many churches are there in Weed?" Weed was my hometown in California, a small mountain community of about thirty-five hundred people.

I started to count and came up with eight. The voice then continued, "Eight pastors who are giving their lives to bring the Lord to that community." Then I clearly heard, "Isn't it right for the Kwatay to have one?"

We never looked back. God went on to impress on us from the Scriptures that He had never chosen the strong or proud or numerous, but He was always concerned with the widow and the orphan and the outcast—those who were small in the world's eyes.

When Steve wrote me, two passages of Scripture immediately came to mind:

...How can they call on Him to save them unless they believe in Him? And how can they believe in Him if they have never heard about Him? And how can they hear about Him unless someone tells them? And how will anyone go and tell them without being sent?

—Romans 10:14–15

After this I saw a vast crowd, too great to count, from every nation and tribe and people and language, standing in front of the throne and before the Lamb. They were clothed in white robes and held palm branches in their hands.

—Revelation 7:9

The Kwatay New Testament was dedicated in 2000, and now there is a church—a church that knows God speaks Kwatay. There is nothing God wants to say to them that He cannot say in Kwatay.

I firmly believe that God will be pleased, and that He already is, to hear a small group of voices gathered around His throne singing *Úsali Atambatun!* ("We praise you, God!") in Kwatay.

The Scriptures in the mother tongue are foundational to the growth and maturity of the Church. Evidence of that can be found around the world—from Senegal to India and beyond.

Manaja was a church planter in India, but after five long years of ministry, he was perplexed. He zealously proclaimed the Good News, but he had to admit that even when he ministered to his own people, "I could never be sure if my message really captured their hearts."

Then he attended a year-long storytelling workshop sponsored by the New India Evangelistic Association and guided by Elizabeth Wilson, a Wycliffe consultant. At the workshop Manaja learned how to craft biblically accurate, culturally relevant Bible stories in his mother tongue, in the oral form that fit his culture especially well.

While he was learning to craft stories, he grasped an immensely important concept: the key to reaching his people was their mother tongue. No wonder they hadn't responded to his teaching! He'd been sharing the Good News in the language of wider communication—not the language they'd grown up with, the one that spoke to the depths of their hearts.

By the time Dallas and I met Manaja at the closing celebration of the workshop, he and his teammates had prepared twenty-five oral Bible stories in their language—all tested with mother tongue speakers and checked by SIL consultants. These were the very first Scripture portions ever translated into their language.

Not long afterward Manaja visited a village where his mother tongue was spoken and invited people to listen to a story. None of them were believers, but within an hour, twenty-five villagers gathered to listen with rapt attention as he narrated the story of creation.

One of those who listened was an eight-year-old boy who'd strayed from his mother. She rushed up just as Manaja finished the story. "What have you been doing?" she demanded of her son.

"Ma, I've been hearing this story from Uncle Manaja!" he responded excitedly.

"Who is he and what has he told you?" she asked. Manaja listened as the boy narrated the story from start to finish.

"That was one of the finest moments in my five-year-old ministry," said Manaja. "Just witnessing how this method and this story in the heart language captured the heart of this young lad, who not only recalled it and repeated it, but also encouraged his mother to discuss it further!"

Faith Comes By Hearing[1] made these Bible stories available on their audio players called Proclaimers, and the recorded stories were also uploaded to the Internet. People listened to them online or downloaded them to their mobile phones, which have flooded the region's rural villages.

---

1 Faith Comes By Hearing is committed to reaching the nations with the Word of God in audio format.

At one meeting one hundred ten men and women from three villages gathered to listen to Proclaimers and learn about God from stories, sermons, and one-on-one mentoring. Seven months after the workshop workers in two districts counted sixty-six new house churches and fifteen hundred believers in regular attendance.

"Without doubt, these lives continue to be impacted as God's Word—in their language for the first time—touches and transforms their communities and their value systems," said Dr. Alexander Philip, director of New India Evangelistic Association.[2]

The Bible stories were just the first step. Almost immediately Manaja and his colleagues went to work on a translation of the Gospel of Luke, with plans to use the book as a script for their own version of the "JESUS" film, and then to continue the translation of more Scriptures.

Step by step God's Word is reaching Manaja's people through the translated Word of God, which has the power to change lives and grow the church into maturity. The same story could be told about each of the seven other people groups for whom Bible stories were prepared at the storytelling workshop.

Loren Cunningham, founder of Youth With A Mission (YWAM), wrote a book with the title, *The Book That Transforms Nations*.[3] In it he argues that the Bible is foundational to every other ministry—including planting churches. I couldn't agree with him more. Throughout Wycliffe's history, we have watched the translated Word undergird and provide impetus to evangelism, discipleship, and church planting, at the same time supporting literacy and other endeavors that minister to the whole person.

---

2 New India Evangelistic Association operates Christian ministries in ten states of India and is committed to reaching out to the unreached and least evangelized people.
3 Loren Cunningham and Janice Rogers, *The Book That Transforms Nations: The Power of the Bible to Change Any Country* (Seattle, WA: YWAM Pub., 2006).

The Bible transforms individuals, communities, and entire countries, setting the context for a mature body of believers, and honoring and glorifying God. When His Word arrives, inevitably a church starts to grow whether that is the intent or not.

Pastor Tama Nicodeme Biesse and his colleagues in Senegal saw results like this when they translated the Gospel of Mark into their mother tongue, Oniyan. It was the first book of the Bible they'd translated, and even before they finished, they saw its power demonstrated in their own lives and in the lives of others around them.

"Because we have translated the Gospel of Mark," Nicodeme said, "we have a clearer understanding of what we have always accepted by faith. We know in our souls a peace and a sense of well-being. Our prayer lives have changed a lot. Our thirst for God's Word has grown so much that we have already done the first draft of the Gospel of Luke in less than a month."

As a result of his translation experience, Nicodeme began to pray in his mother tongue. His pastoral studies had been in French and his Bible was in French, so he'd always expressed spiritual truths in that language—whether he was talking to other people or to God. But the translation process was all about finding Oniyan ways to express biblical truths. Once he'd done that, he was able to pray in Oniyan, and the result was a new sense of communion with God. He found that what he could never express in French, he could freely share with God in his heart language.

Confident that he could express biblical terms in Oniyan, Nicodeme also began to preach in that language. He was impressed that for the first time, people in the congregation could clearly understand his sermons. After each sermon, they would review the main points with each other and even share them with their unbelieving neighbors.

Other members of the translation team also felt God working in their lives. Gerard, who was not an emotional man by nature, felt himself becoming more sensitive to the spiritual needs of those around him and more willing to share the Good News. During the checking of Mark, the team talked with a village chief who told them that his heart's desire was to see his people saved by Jesus Christ. "Please don't abandon us," he said. "If you do, my people will be condemned to become adherents of another religion, even though we are convinced that we cannot find truth there." Gerard almost wept—surprising himself with the depth of his compassion for these people.

Another colleague, Jeremie, who joined the translation team as an unbeliever, met Jesus through translating the Gospel of Mark. His life changed so much that members of his family asked him what had made the difference. His answer was to share the Scriptures with them, conducting a translation-testing session in their home. As the team read from Mark's Gospel, Jeremie's brothers, sisters, mother, and his father's second wife were significantly touched. "How can we find out more about this Jesus?" they asked. "We've always heard about Him, but we still don't know Him."

So the translation team planned a showing of the "JESUS" film. Huge numbers of people came from all around, and several people gave their lives to the Lord, including the chief of a nearby village. As a result, Nicodeme and the rest of the team began holding a service in his village every Saturday. "A new church has been born in this village," said Nicodeme, "though we hadn't planned it—at least not this year!"

Nicodeme expressed deep gratitude for his coworkers, especially Jim and Patricia Winters, and for Christians in other places who gave financially so Oniyan speakers could have the Gospel of Mark. Because of their partnership, he said, the Good News was beginning to replace ceremonies previously dedicated to evil spirits and, as he put it, "The kingdom of God is advancing far into the African bush."

As the Oniyan team enthusiastically embarked on further translation, Nicodeme could not help exclaiming, "Glory to God who makes His Word powerful and effective in our midst."

11

EVERYONE HAS THE RIGHT TO HAVE THE BIBLE

When Jesus wanted people to know the extent to which God would go to reach the last "one," He told three stories that are recorded in Luke chapter 15: the lost sheep, the lost coin, and the lost son. No one is too small or insignificant to merit God's attention; no one is beyond the reach of His love. Many have followed the example in these parables as they reach out to communities in remote parts of the world.

The Cacua are a small group of people who live in the rainforest of southeastern Colombia. As a result of the work of Marilyn Cathcart, Lois Lowers, and several Cacua translators, they now have the Scriptures in their language.

Though few in number, the Cacua's influence as Bible teachers has spread well beyond their language boundaries. Their love for God's Word and their knowledge of the Word are well known, and they are much in demand as teachers at the semiannual Christian conferences held among the neighboring Cubeo people. If they were to respond to all the invitations they receive from the Cubeos, they could spend their entire year traveling from village to village teaching the Word.

They've even gone to Brazil—a five-day trip each way—to teach the Word at Bible conferences. On those occasions, Emi (the first Cacua Bible translator) taught in Cacua, with one of his fellow villagers translating into Cubeo. Then another person translated from Cubeo into Curripaco, and finally someone else translated from Curripaco into Portuguese.

In addition to being Bible teachers, they're also evangelists. They've discovered a way to take a cultural event and turn it into a tool for evangelization. Traditionally the people groups in the area have held all-night drinking parties, punctuated by loud fights and machete swinging. Now the Cacua believers hold their own all-night parties— with funny programs and crazy costumes, as well as singing, Bible study, and times of testimony. They invite unbelievers to the parties and show them how to have fun without getting drunk. Then they use the opportunity to actively witness to them.

Though the Cacua are leaders today, it hasn't always been that way. Before the translated Word of God reached them, the people around them viewed them with contempt. In fact they were servants—even slaves—of the surrounding villages. At any time they could be ordered by their "owners" to clear a field, carry a load, or do whatever else needed to be done. Being a Cacua was to be the lowest of the low—to be truly marginalized. Not anymore.

What changed them? Not people. Not crusades. It was the Word of God, set free among them in the language they best understood. Access to that tool changed their hearts and enabled them to make dramatic changes in their own lives and in the lives of those to whom they now minister.

The Bible has a lot to say about God's special love for the poor, the downtrodden, and the oppressed. I believe that He is pleased when marginalized people are offered the Scriptures in their language. Six hundred years ago John Wycliffe translated the Scriptures for the marginalized people of his day, the English peasants. We honor God when we choose to say with Wycliffe, "Everyone has a right, even peasants, to hear and understand the Word of God." It changes the direction of their lives—not just for eternity, but also for the here and now.

There isn't anything God wants to say that He cannot say in the everyday language that people speak. One of the places where His message has been clearly understood and enthusiastically celebrated is an unpretentious village in Southeast Asia where the Ketengban language is spoken.

One day a single-engine plane circled and landed in this remote village. Translators Andrew and Anne Sims stepped out and were immediately surrounded by several hundred Ketengban men and women—all dressed in full celebratory dress with feathered headdresses; some had bones in their noses and plugs in their earlobes. Brandishing bows and arrows, hooting, chanting, and dancing, they swirled in and around Andrew and Anne, honoring them by draping net bags around their necks.

Andrew and Anne were caught completely off-guard. Even though they were responsible for the Ketengban translation project, and this was Anne's first visit since the New Testament dedication eleven years earlier, they hadn't expected such an exuberant welcome. They were further baffled when they noticed that not everyone was celebrating.

Off to the edge of the crowd stood a somber group of about eight young men. Like everyone else, they were dressed in full traditional regalia, but they were also covered in white mud from head to toe. They stood expressionless and silent, never moving, never joining in the celebration.

The elders explained:

Today we celebrate your return, Andrew and Anne—you who brought God's words to us in our own language. But we don't want to forget what life was like before we had the Word, so we asked these young men to cover themselves with mud and to stand apart, silent and somber. They represent the lives of all of us before we understood God's words to us. We were like dead men walking. We didn't know God or His Son. We lived in guilt and fear and constant warfare, always under the power of the evil spirits, who terrified us and caused us to fear one another as well.

Now we are alive in Christ and free from our dark past. We are insiders, part of God's family—no longer outsiders silently watching from afar. But our children don't remember what it was like to be outsiders and walk as dead men, because they were born after the coming of God's words. We want them to understand our past so they will fully value what they have with Jesus and will always give thanks to God. We older people don't want to forget how much God has changed us either!

The Ketengban have it right: Against a background of darkness, light shines more brightly. If you don't have your own memories of the darkness and fear outside of God's family, I'd encourage you to tuck away the Ketengban's story for those occasions when you need a fresh appreciation for all that God has done.

12

THE VALUE OF HOLISTIC MINISTRY

When Dallas and I arrived in Cameroon in 1987, a pilot project was underway in cooperation with the Cameroonian government. The project was founded on the belief that if you taught children to read and write in their mother tongue first, and then "bridged" them into literacy in a language of wider communication—either French or English—they would be more successful in school. The program proved to be very successful, as it has been in other places around the world.

This approach to education was started by SIL in Peru many years ago when the government was more interested in children learning to read and write in Spanish than in their mother tongue. Bilingual education proved to be highly successful. Now labeled "multilingual education," or sometimes "mother tongue first" or "first language education," the approach continues to work.

Longitudinal studies show that children who have been enrolled in these programs, and who are first taught to read and write in the language of their birth, bridge more easily into education in a national language. They stay in school longer and are more successful in their studies.[1]

Mofu is a language spoken in Northern Cameroon. The New Testament is available now in Mofu, and so is a program of multilingual education in schools. A recent report showed that students who followed this mother-tongue-first approach to learning to read and write had a passing rate of 99 percent on the end-of-primary-school exams. Schools *not* using the mother tongue as the means of teaching the early grades had a maximum of 49 percent passing.

Multilingual education in a Bai classroom.

I've seen multilingual education replicated all over the world. When I have visited schools in places like Cameroon, the Philippines, and China, I have been amazed to observe the contrast between mother-

1 An Editor's Note in the *AfricaFocus Bulletin* says: "…In a new report released in June 2010, researchers from UNESCO and the Association for the Development of Education in Africa challenge the common assumptions in many African countries that mother language instruction is impractical or counter-productive. To the contrary, a review of recent research and practice indicates, multilingual education including mother-language instruction into later years of schooling, as well as an international language, produces better results than an early transition to exclusive use of the international language. Multilingualism, the authors contend, is an asset that Africa must foster for practical reasons as well as reasons of cultural pride." —William Minter, ed., "Africa: Multilingual Education Pays Off," *AfricaFocus Bulletin*, July 20, 2010, http://www.africafocus.org/docs10/educ1007.php.

tongue-first classrooms and classrooms where the mother tongue was not used. Kids in classes using their mother tongue were more involved in the learning process than their peers being taught only in French, English, or Mandarin. In the traditional classes kids sat in rows and learned—or memorized—the lessons on the chalkboard. But in the non-traditional, mother-tongue-first classes, the kids were animated and interactive with the teacher.

Most language communities today exist in the context of other languages, and over time more and more governments have changed their language policies to include a multilingual approach to education.

Recently, an article in *Global Times,* a Chinese publication, said:

School is hard enough when you are a kid, but imagine if you did not even speak the language you are being taught in. That is the case for millions of children in Yunnan Province, which boasts the greatest ethnic diversity in China, containing 25 of the country's 55 ethnic minority groups. While most kids speak their mother tongue at home, they often find themselves struggling in school, where classes are taught in Putonghua [the de facto national language of the People's Republic of China]....

The Research Institute of Southwestern Minority Languages and Cultures in Guizhou University…found that 60 percent of the students in their bilingual project among the Dong people in Guizhou finished junior middle school and attended senior middle school, much higher than the 10 percent seen in the past.

. . .Yang Jimin, the project manager from the education bureau of Jianchuan, said the students showed significant improvement in their test results. The school used to rank at the bottom in the township, but now has moved up to the mid-level.

"We also found that kids who learned their mother tongue first are much better at learning Putonghua and show much better progress in cognitive development," said Yang.[2]

These projects are being conducted with the cooperation of SIL.[3]

Multilingual educational programs expand the horizons and capabilities of individuals within a community, providing the means by which the quality of life for both individuals and the community can be improved.

For a large number of language communities struggling under the weight of poverty and disease, the first step—the foundational step—toward alleviating poverty is having their language in written form. When linguist/translators come alongside mother tongue speakers to help them develop their languages, their first project is often working together to create an alphabet that fits the sound structure of the language. Once there is an alphabet, there can be books and literacy—first in the mother tongue and then in a language of wider communication.

Literacy and education create opportunities that help communities deal with social justice issues and combat the spread of diseases like HIV, AIDS and malaria. We know that teaching people to read is one of the main things that will help lift them out of poverty.[4] I've heard it said that teaching a mother to read is more effective than putting a doctor in a community (she will be proactive; the doctor is reactive). Statistics support that a child born to a mother who can read is exponentially more likely to survive past age five than a child born to a mother who cannot read.[5]

---

2 Xuyang Jingjing, "Languages on Life Support," *The Global Times*, September 5, 2012, http://www.globaltimes.cn/content/731289.shtml.

3 For more information on multilingual education and the work of SIL, see http://www.sil.org/literacy/multi.htm.

4 Dana Robert, director of the Center for Global Christianity and Mission at Boston University, quoted by Andrea Palpant Dilley, "The Surprising Discovery About Those Colonialist Proselytizing Missionaries," *Christianity Today*, January/February 2014.

5 Unesco.org. "Education Counts Because It Reduces Child Mortality." http://www.unesco.org/new/fileadmin/MULTIMEDIA/HQ/ED/GMR/pdf/gmr2010/MDG-book4.pdf.

On the way to his office one day, Pastor Timothy Bandirana, co-ordinator of the literacy and Scripture use team for the Bwisi of Uganda, stopped at a school for young children between the ages of four and eight. Tucking a few Scripture posters under his arm,[6] he went in to visit the headmistress.

"Could I encourage you to teach your students how to read in Bwisi?" he asked.

"No," said the headmistress. "These children are too young to learn to read the local language."

"But this is their own language," said Timothy. "How can you expect them to understand what you are teaching them in English if they do not first understand in their own language?" Two pupils came into the office just then, and Timothy turned to them. "Do you know how to read these words in Bwisi?"

The boy, whose name was Ntamuhira, replied, "Somebody teaches Bwisi literacy classes at my home. I always attend these classes in the evening and I can read the words on that poster." The girl, Irene, said, "My mother always teaches me how to read the book about Kande[7] in Bwisi."

The headmistress listened as the children confidently read the posters: "Jesus said, 'Follow me'" (Mark 1:17) and "Love your neighbor as you love yourself" (Mark 12:31).

Impressed, she quickly changed her mind and asked for a supply of the posters, saying, "It is difficult for the children to memorize verses in English. English words soon disappear out of their minds.

---

6 The Scripture posters were colored by children in the United States, using resources from Wycliffe's free curriculum for children, and mailed to Uganda. The curriculum is available at www.wycliffe.org.

7 ScriptureEngagement.org. "Kande's Story." http://www.scripture-engagement.org/content/kandes-story.

But in their own language, even though the verse on paper might disappear, the words remain in their minds."

When you think about it, this isn't just about children reading and writing their mother tongue—this is about something much larger. These children represent the future of their community—the future of the church in the Bwisi community. It's a church that knows fear and heartache because of a high concentration of HIV and AIDS, but it's also a church that knows hope.

The Bwisi now have an alphabet, the first Scriptures in their language, and *Kande's Story,* which addresses the issues surrounding AIDS in a culturally and Scripturally appropriate way.

Young Bwisi speakers reading *Kande's Story* together.

Kande's Story—now translated into almost two hundred languages around the world—is about a twelve-year-old African girl who grieves over her father and mother, who died of AIDS. She and her five siblings, now orphans, must fend for themselves, facing many problems and dangers just to survive. Various people in their community, especially local church members, minister to their needs.

Irene's mother was a victim of HIV and has now died because of AIDS. This may be one reason why she taught her daughter to read *Kande's Story*. By the time Irene was eight years old, she was an orphan and responsible for her younger brother, Tumwesige. "I'm going to love him and take care of him, just like Kande cared for her siblings," Irene told Pastor Timothy. "That's what my mother told me to do."

With their early exposure to literacy in their mother tongue, Bwisi children are equipped to read the translated Scriptures—the solid foundation and future of the Bwisi church. And with the Kande storybook and community-wide seminars, they are better equipped at an early age to deal with things that most of their agemates in the United States have not yet needed to think about.

I witnessed firsthand what was happening among the Bwisi people when I had the privilege of attending a graduation ceremony in Bundibugyo, Uganda. Sixty Bwisi people from the Democratic Republic of the Congo and Uganda had completed a training seminar based on *Kande's Story*. All of the participants were HIV positive. Many shared how the training had helped them see their illness in terms of God's perspective and how they had learned to help others avoid the disease.

Seminars like this one help HIV-infected people live with the disease. They learn to communicate more openly with their families, seek reconciliation in relationships, make wills, and help their children prepare for the future.

What's amazing is that, according to the testimonies I heard, the seminars also help HIV-infected people find hope. Through studies in the Scriptures, the participants gain knowledge and assurance of God's forgiveness and eternal life. "This kind of seminar brings us closer to God," said one man.

At the seminar I visited, three people came into a relationship with God for the first time, and I was told this is quite common. Along with new and renewed relationships with God, the seminar participants experience repaired relationships with spouses and families. Rejection and fear are replaced with acceptance and love.

Kande seminars also help pastors and other church members learn how to support HIV and AIDS victims better. One pastor said, "Meeting to read *Kande's Story*, you can really sympathize. You can cry real tears. You learn to care. You learn to prevent AIDS. You learn to be faithful to your spouse....Let the training continue!"

The fact that the Bwisi people are learning about HIV and AIDS in their own language—rather than English—is tremendously important. "This Kande book is helping me to teach about AIDS," said one man. "It is in my mother tongue, and it is understood well by others, unlike other materials in English that many cannot understand."

One of my most meaningful memories of the graduation event is the moment when a seminar participant approached me with a gift to say thank you for Wycliffe USA's contribution to the program. Presenting me with a small handmade bag, he said, "Though I am poor, I am not too poor to say thank you. I wanted to give something to the man who sends funds to help us have books like *Kande's Story*. This book was written for me! Please keep up the good work."

I am increasingly grateful that God has given us the opportunity to minister in His name—in the languages He created—to the Bwisi and others who need practical help with diseases like HIV and who need to hear the Good News about Jesus Christ. It's an injustice for people not to have information they need—access to the Bible, health-related materials, and more. When people hear information vital to their well-being in their own language, they respond more easily and with deeper understanding.

While languages exist in a context, so does the work of Bible translation. Many times, giving attention to a people's physical and emotional needs precedes Bible translation. This is only natural because when caring people get to know people in need, God nudges them to do what they can to meet that need.

I mentioned earlier that I spent a few days with Terrill and Amber Schrock in Uganda. You'll remember that they're the team for whom Wycliffe staff members Dave and Linda Marcy are praying (see chapter 6). They work with the Ik people who live in the northeastern corner of the country on the edge of the Rift Valley. Terrill is doing language development, including Bible translation, while Amber supports him through health care and community development projects.

When I first met them, Amber was providing health care in the back of a storage building behind their home in Kaabong. She told me she usually saw thirty people each day, three times a week, but sometimes she saw up to sixty patients in a single day. If a patient was too sick to come to Amber's clinic, she went and picked them up and took them to a hospital.

While I was there, two of my traveling companions rode along with Amber when she picked up a woman in labor, rushed her to the hospital, and helped deliver a healthy baby!

Why does Amber do this work? She says she wants to bless people. "My dad taught us that one way to follow God was through serving other people. After high school, I pursued a career that would let me minister to people's physical needs," she explains. She also sees her service as a way of gaining acceptance into the Ik community. She believes that providing basic health care and identifying publicly with the Ik people will help her and Terrill establish rapport with the Ik.

Beyond that, she recognizes the validity of ministering to the whole person. "We really do believe that people need to meet basic needs before they will be open to Bible translation," she says. "They are thinking about hunger, shelter—not 'Who is this man named Jesus?'

Once these basic needs are met, then the Ik people will start thinking, 'Who is God?'"

We in Wycliffe have traditionally presented ourselves as Bible translators by choice and as literacy specialists, linguists, researchers, and community development workers more out of necessity. We've talked about spiritual results, but we haven't said much about other kinds of results—at least as an organization. As individuals, we've kept our partners informed of our ministry to the whole person, but as an organization we haven't usually said too much about it.

Certainly Bible translation is and always will be our primary focus. It's the particular focus that God has entrusted to us and others for reaching the nations, and I would not want to dilute anyone's understanding of who we are.

But Bible translation has never been done in a vacuum, and the results have never been measured purely in spiritual terms. It's always been part of a larger package; it's always included ministry to a community's physical, social, and economic needs. And that ministry—now called holistic ministry—is an increasingly important part of the story. Meeting the needs of the whole person is a very high value for us. This is not something new that we need to add to our Bible translation ministry; it's always been there.

When we fight Bible poverty, we are also fighting physical poverty. Wycliffe's vision is for every man, woman, and child to hear the Good News in the language and form they understand best; the vision does not specifically address physical poverty. However, Bible translation—and the accompanying language development, including literacy—is often the starting point for solutions to some of the world's most pressing humanitarian issues. It's foundational to other ministries.

Many are surprised to discover what happens when Bible translation takes place in a community: literacy, education, improved health care, access to clean water, improved human rights and government relations, community empowerment, and more. All of these advances, of course, combat poverty.

Wycliffe and our partners believe that everyone has a right to have access to the Scriptures and the opportunity to know the One who is the source of truth and eternal life. We also believe that everyone should have access to information and education that gives them the means to overcome painful and oppressive conditions in this life. And it can all start with Bible translation.

When "God loved the world so much that he gave his one and only Son" (John 3:16a), He did it in response to the fear and hopelessness of a world marred by sin. When His Son died on the cross, He opened the way for reconciliation with God and renewed hope and joy. It is our amazing privilege to share in this ministry of reconciliation by helping people the world over gain access to God's Word in their mother tongue—their best opportunity to understand this eternal truth—and learn to apply it to their spiritual and physical needs.

THE FINISH LINE

13

DREAMS AND VISIONS

Do you believe in dreams and visions? Or more specifically, does your worldview permit God to use your dreams to give you vision and direction? This is something to be careful with, for sure, but my experience is that He can and sometimes does give direction to us by invading our dreams, often giving us a vision much larger than ourselves.

When you google "Cameron Townsend," the principal founder of Wycliffe Bible Translators, and then look at images, many of the photos you find show him in the "sunset" of his life—in other words, in his seventies and eighties. It's easy to forget that Townsend was a young man once and that God gave him the Bible translation vision when he was young.

A few years ago I commissioned a painting of Townsend based on a photograph of him in his twenties, and I gave it to the Townsend family, presenting it to his daughter, Grace Townsend Goreth. When Grace saw it, she cried. "That's Daddy when he first had a vision for worldwide Bible translation," she said.

That says a great deal about Townsend—he became focused early and he maintained his focus throughout his entire life! When he launched this worldwide effort labeled "Wycliffe Bible Translators," he thought there might be five hundred languages in the world. Though more and more languages were discovered as the years went by, he never lost sight of his vision that the last one would be reached!

Cameron Townsend in his twenties—already focused on Bible translation. Painting by Michael Harrar of Wycliffe USA.

We know today that there are close to seven thousand languages! We also know that while Bible translation has gone on for hundreds, even thousands of years, the pace at which translation is taking place today is unprecedented. The number of people with access to Scripture they can understand is higher than it has ever been, and more people have more access to the Good News than ever before in history.

In chapter 5 I told the story of translator Lee Bramlett and the Hdi people, who needed the right word for God's love. One night in a dream God prompted Lee to try a form of the Hdi word for love that he thought should exist, but that he'd never heard used. Thinking about John 3:16, he asked the translation committee, "Could God *dvu* people?"

Their response was complete silence, followed by quiet tears. Finally they said, "Do you know what this would mean? This would mean that God kept on loving us over and over, millennia after millennia, while all that time we rejected His great love. He is compelled to love us, even though we have sinned more than any people."

God had encoded the story of His unconditional love right into their language, but no one recognized it until God spoke to Lee in a dream. Now that word is part of their Scriptures, continually revealing His love to Hdi readers. Someday the last word of the last bit of Scripture for the last community will be translated, and everyone will be able to understand the story of God's unconditional love—and of the Cross, which changes everything. God uses the unique resources of each language to tell His story, and sometimes He reveals these resources through dreams.

Kenneth Pike[1] is one of our "heroes" in Wycliffe. He was one of our pioneer linguists, beginning his study of languages in 1935, and he is still considered one of the most gifted and prominent linguists ever born. Brilliant as he was, he was stymied by a linguistic secret in the Mexican language he was studying. San Miguel el Grande Mixteco is a tonal language—a language in which changing the tone (pitch) of a word can change its meaning even when everything else remains the same. Pike knew he could not adequately speak or write the language until he understood how the tone system worked.

George Cowan, president emeritus of Wycliffe, tells the story.

Pike was so frustrated that he was ready to quit! He'd get a whole bunch of words written down and the next day he'd come back

---

1 To read more about Kenneth Pike, go to http://www.wycliffe.org/about/ourhistory/kennethpike.aspx.

to review them only to find the tones seemed to have changed. He heard the tones quite differently, and the same word seemed to change tones in different contexts and combinations with other words. He didn't know whether his writing of them had been wrong, or his hearing was playing tricks on him from one day to the next, or the speakers varied in how they would pronounce them.

Finally, in desperation, he took a day off to fast and pray. He made his way up a mountain where he could be alone with God. There he asked the Lord to give him a solution to his problem. He dared to ask that the solution would not only meet his own problem, but also similar problems the other linguists of his group were encountering elsewhere in Mexico.

All day long he thought and prayed. He turned over in his mind all he knew about the baffling tone fluctuations in Mixtec. He thought about a statement he'd heard by Dr. Edward Sapir, a leading linguist of the day. Dr. Sapir had said that words in a tonal language needed to be analyzed in relationship to each other. He needed to choose a sentence to use as a "frame" and substitute words, one after another, into the same spot in the sentence. By sunset, tired and hungry, he went back down the mountain, eager to try out the new idea.

The next morning when his Mixtec coworker came, Ken gave him a sentence and asked him to substitute lists of words into it. The repetition of the same frame helped to stabilize Ken's hearing and made it easier to hear the differences in tone between the substituted words. By the time he'd listened to the same lists several times, comparing them to different frames, he began to see that in some instances, tones changed depending on the words around them.

He also learned that the Mixtecs might change the level of a sentence according to their moods, but the relative pitches of the words within the sentence would not change. Before long he was able to determine that each syllable of Mixtec was spoken on either a high, mid, or low tone, and that certain words would change the pitch of the words around them in predictable ways.

God had given Pike the key—not only to Mixtec, but also to other tonal languages as well. This solution is still used today to "unlock" languages that use tone to change meaning. Pike always attributed this discovery to God's revelation, not his own ingenuity.

God also spoke into the dream of a software engineer in Papua New Guinea—with dramatic results. Bruce Waters woke up one morning in November 1999 with an idea that seemed like a half-dream, but as he gradually became alert, he realized that God had given him a significant key to accelerate the task of Bible translation. Using that key, he developed a software program called Adapt It.

Adapt It allows a bilingual translator to take advantage of the work already done on one translation to produce a second translation in a closely related language.

The translator begins with a completed New Testament in one language, and works through the text word by word and phrase by phrase. Whenever he or she comes to a word or phrase that isn't used in the second language, (s)he replaces it with the appropriate expression, and Adapt It stores that information. As the translator approaches each new word or phrase, Adapt It compares it to those already stored. If it finds a match with a unique translation, it automatically inserts the translation and moves ahead to the next word. The translator has the option of accepting that translation or entering a second translation. The next time the word or phrase occurs, the program prompts the translator to decide whether to use one of the translations already stored or to enter yet another one. As more words and phrases are stored, the pace picks up, and a first draft can be completed very quickly.

Like any first draft, the translation has to be carefully checked with mother tongue speakers and consultants, but Adapt It cuts many years off the time it would otherwise have taken to complete it.

Bruce says, "To me it is more than a coincidence that in the year that the Lord was guiding our leadership to formulate the Vision 2025,[2] he led someone to develop a bit of technology that could significantly help in achieving the vision."

On other occasions God has prepared a people group for the coming of His Word through dreams, as he did the Borana people of Kenya.

One evening, at the end of a hot desert day, a small group of Borana people—nomadic cattle herders—sat down under the stars to share news and stories. As Wycliffe translators Jim and Dorothea Lander joined them, an elder began to speak:

Long, long ago the Borana people had a Book of God. We called it our Boogi Waqa and everyone had a copy. We read it often to learn how to please God. But as the years passed, our books began to wear out until eventually only one remained—the prized possession of an old, old grandfather.

Those were years of drought, and our people relentlessly battled for survival. Day after day the old man and his family took their cattle out on long searches for grass and water. One day they left behind a cow too weak to keep up with them. Nosing around for food while no one watched, she came upon the last Boogi Waqa. . .and devoured it! When the old man came home that

---

2 Vision 2025 is Wycliffe's vision that all language communities needing a Bible translation will have a program in progress by the year 2025.

night, he found only a few pieces of leather binding scattered on the ground. Great sadness filled the camp.

That night the old man slept fitfully and dreamt that an angel appeared to him. The angel promised that after many years, God would send their book back to them. "Watch for a strange man from a faraway country," said the angel. "When he comes, treat him well, for he will bring back your Boogi Waqa."

Many years later the first missionaries came into Borana land. Some of you remember them. They tried to learn our language, and one of them actually wrote a book he said came from God, but we could not read it.

The elder paused, and then with a long sigh, he concluded: "Now, my children, we still wait for the Boogi Waqa."

A few weeks later, Jim and Dorothea entertained some Borana men in their home. After dinner and several cups of sweet, creamy tea, a man named Galgalo picked up the Lander children's English Picture Bible. Galgalo could read English because he'd served in the Kenyan Air Force. He read the story of the Tower of Babel in English and then told the Borana men what it said in their own language.

Together they looked at the pictures in the Bible and exclaimed, "Look, these men dress just like we do, with flowing robes and turbans! They pack their camels like we do! And this desert looks just like ours!"

Galgalo turned to Jim and asked, "Is this a Borana book? Is it … could it be … the Boogi Waqa?"

"Yes," said Jim. "This is the Boogi Waqa."

Silently the men stared at Jim and Dorothea. Slowly they turned their gaze back to the book. Long into the night they explored the book, examining the pictures and listening to Galgalo read. Eventually they came to a picture of the Israelites in the Old Testament sacrificing a lamb.

The men told Jim, "Our fathers taught us that the Boogi Waqa told how to sacrifice a lamb so that God would forgive our sins. And sure enough, here it is in this Boogi Waqa! We still do our animal sacrifices, but some of the missionaries say we should stop. Why is that?"

His heart pounding, Jim took the Bible and turned to Hebrews, chapter 10. He was still learning the language, but with Galgalo's help, he explained that God sent His Son, Jesus, to be the perfect sacrifice for sin. They no longer needed to sacrifice lambs each year because now they could find forgiveness of sin and eternal life by putting their trust in Jesus, who died for their sins once and for all!

Health concerns later sent the Landers back to the States, but a Borana man, David Diida, drew on their linguistic and orthographic research to spearhead a revision of the Bible and a very successful literacy program. Countless groups of believers now read their own Book of God all across Northern Kenya.

Dorothea says, "I believe God placed the Boogi Waqa story in Borana history and preserved it in their oral culture so that many years after the original book disappeared, men would seek after God and find in Him eternal life by reading their new Boogi Waqa."

Ralph Winters, founder of the U.S. Center for World Missions, told *Mission Frontiers* readers, "The Bible itself is now clearly out of control in many parts of the world. Wycliffe Bible Translators are right: once people get the Bible in their own language, you can readily expect what in many cases will be explosive growth of 'faith movements to Christ.'"[3]

---

3 Ralph D. Winters, ed., "Are We Accelerating or Inhibiting Movements to Christ?" editorial, *Missions Frontiers*, September 1, 2006, https://www.missionfrontiers.org/issue/article/editorial-comment15.

An explosive growth of faith movements to Christ … the Bible changing lives and communities in ways no missionary can—or wants to—control … a spreading hunger for the Word of God. Yes, in more and more places, speakers of minority languages are reaching out for the Word of God. They want it in their own language, and they're eager to be part of the process. Vision 2025 is both a cause for and a response to this growing momentum.

Vision 2025 is huge—but so is God's ability to realize it. God loves the speakers of those last languages, and He's going to see that they get His Word—by whatever creative means He chooses.

And sometimes He chooses to use dreams and visions.

THE FINISH LINE

14

THE POWER OF TECHNOLOGY

I used to chuckle when I heard Loren Cunningham, the founder of Youth With A Mission (YWAM) say, "God created the passenger jet airplane so that YWAM could evangelize the world!" I don't laugh any more. I think God has given us great advances in technology to use to complete the Bible translation task and to create access to Scripture in unprecedented ways.

My colleague, Mundara Muturi, Africa Area director for the Wycliffe Global Alliance, is Kenyan. He calls attention to these technological changes by holding up his cell phone and exclaiming: "This has changed everything in Africa!"

Mundara is right. I remember my own experiences in Africa, living there years ago without a cell phone. Now almost everyone has one, and I marvel at how the world has changed for my friends and colleagues working there—both Africans and expats. Whereas Dallas and I used to have to sign up to use the one landline phone in our offices in Yaoundé, Cameroon, now many of our colleagues can call their families back in the United States right from their remote locations in villages across the country. When we were in Cameroon recently, we had a cell signal, and I was able to update my Facebook page as we drove between villages. Mundara uses his phone to transfer money to his parents, who live in a remote part of Kenya.

Pastors from Myanmar see the Bible on a phone for the first time.

I'm old enough to remember printed encyclopedias, but I can't remember the last time I used one. I now use Google and Wikipedia. Paper files? I use electronic files and store them in "the cloud." Desktops and laptops? Many of us use tablets and smartphones. When was the last time you used a payphone? How about a keyboard or a mouse? I love my touch screen—oh, and speech recognition. Cash, checks, and debit cards? They're still around, but I just paid for a cup of coffee using my phone.

My son-in-law, Paul Yoo, is one of the founders of Mistral Mobile. This software technology guarantees secure transactions on any phone, at any price point, and over any operator network, without the consumer having a data connection. All that is needed is a voice and SMS (text messaging) connection. It eliminates the barriers preventing banks, mobile operators, and financial service providers from serving the billions of people in need of financial services in emerging markets. The company is marketing their product in the developing world.

Paul told me, "The mobile Internet ramp rate is staggering. And payments are the basic infrastructure necessary to allow any m-commerce to take place. I think of it as building roads. But once you've built the roads, you can build on top—and it's the second order once those 'roads' have been built that in many ways makes the business opportunity much, much more interesting…."

I now carry my "Bible" everywhere I go—on my smartphone and tablet. When I mark a passage or insert a note, everything immediately syncs across three platforms: smartphone, tablet, and computer. I love it!

We're living in a period of time when we can reimagine everything, and God can use any of these emerging technologies for His own purposes.

Imagine boarding a plane in Dallas, Texas, and heading for Southeast Asia to visit the Yawa people. You will travel for several days by plane, then board a truck and journey into lush green mountains on a deeply rutted, often muddy road. If recent rains have caused landslides to cover the road, you may need to continue on foot. Eventually you'll come to a small village nestled into a mountain valley, where the local language people speak is Yawa.

In the past the people in this village worshipped in the "official" language of the country, not the language of their home and heart. But things have changed dramatically since the arrival of Scriptures in the Yawa language!

The availability of Bible portions—and now the complete New Testament—has had a huge impact on the way Yawa people worship and on their understanding of the message of the Gospel. If you ask if anyone preaches from the Yawa Scriptures, you'll hear things like, "Elder Sefnat does all the time." When you find Sefnat, he might show you two small worn books protected by brown paper covers—translations of John's writings, Acts, and nine epistles which he's treasured since before the New Testament was completed and published. Tucked into the pages are little slips of paper with dated sermon notes, references to Scripture passages in those two little books, and unpublished verses that the Yawa translator handwrote for him while the translation was still in process.

Continuing your walk through the village, you might stop by a certain thatched-roof home and ask if anyone there reads from the Scriptures in Yawa. The residents will probably point to a bearded old man and say, "Grandfather Bertasar read to us this morning. He told us how to apply it to our lives, too."

Walking on, you'll come to the village church. If you had visited here in 2009 or 2010, you would have encountered an amazing scene. In this very remote village, where there is still neither electricity nor phone service, translator Mandowen Rawai spent his days at a laptop computer. A dozen people often clustered closely around him, listening as he read a Bible passage in Yawa aloud. The volunteer reviewers would enthusiastically discuss it, looking for ways to improve awkward or unclear sentences. When they were satisfied with the way it sounded, Mandowen would revise it on his computer. Then he would log onto the Internet, and using the send/receive function of his specially designed translation software, he would "sync" his draft.

Halfway around the world, in Arlington, Texas, Wycliffe translator Linda Jones would get up in the morning, sync up her computer, and find his revisions. She would check to make sure the meaning was still faithful to the original and send back suggestions for the next round of discussions.

Working together long distance was not new to Linda and Mandowen. They'd been doing it for seventeen years—ever since Linda and her husband, Larry, needed to leave the village so Larry could take on a series of leadership roles with Wycliffe. Before the Internet connection, Scripture drafts went back and forth by mail and in hand-carried packets. Linda and Larry made trips to the village; and Mandowen made trips out of the village. Always God helped them find a way forward, but Linda and Larry thought they had reached the end of the road when it came to the final revision process.

"We did not see how we could finish the final revisions to the New Testament without greater community involvement," says Linda. "It just looked impossible. I could not go there for any length of time, and they could not come here."

Linda Jones with Mandowen and other Yawa people learning to use their new BGAN satellite receiver.

Then, in early 2009, a new geostationary satellite started circling the equator. Wycliffe's IT specialists were ready! Just two weeks after the satellite went into service, they carried a computer and a small satellite device to the village, showed Mandowen how to connect to the satellite, and taught him to use OurWord—a software program for translators created by Wycliffe IT specialist John Wimbish.

It was just in time! With Mandowen and the village reviewers working in Southeast Asia, and Linda working in Texas, they finished the final revisions of the New Testament. Today the Yawa have their own published copies of the Scriptures, which they can use to learn about God and grow in Him.

Was the launching of the satellite at this strategic time a coincidence? I don't think so. This was all part of God's plan for the Yawa.

These advances in technology and the ability to communicate over great distances provide Bible translators with new tools to increase the speed and quality of their translations. Translators are taking advantage of this progress, leveraging the new tools for the benefit of those still waiting for Scripture in their own language. With the commitment of national colleagues like Mandowen, all of this rolls up into the greatest acceleration of the pace of Bible translation ever witnessed by the Church.

Now imagine a database containing all the Scriptures in the world, and software that allows Scripture providers to access this data and make it available on smartphones anywhere in the world. It's happening!

Every Tribe Every Nation (ETEN)[1] is a donor-led partnership between three major ministries that are in the process of uploading Scripture texts to a database called The Digital Bible Library. Wycliffe, SIL, and The Seed Company[2] are part of the alliance, as are The American Bible Society/United Bible Societies, and Biblica. Along with their partners, these organizations account for 90 percent of the Bible translations in the world. All are uploading texts to the database so that qualified ministries can have access to them.

---

1 Every Tribe Every Nation, "World's Three Major Bible Ministries Partner with Philanthropists to Create The Digital Bible Library," news release, December 13, 2012, Every Tribe Every Nation, http://www.everytribeeverynation.org/Websites/eten/files/Content/4096494/etendbllaunch-releasefinal.pdf.

2 The Seed Company was launched by Wycliffe Bible Translators in 1993 with a mandate to accelerate Bible translation. Today The Seed Company is working with several hundred local translators who are leading the translation process in more than four hundred Bible translation projects. These translators are responding to the local churches' and ministries' need to make Scripture available more quickly for church planting and discipleship.

By collecting texts into one easy-to-access location, The Digital Bible Library will make Scriptures readily available to Christian organizations, ministries, and missionaries, enabling them to share God's Word with those they serve in languages and formats that allow these communities to engage effectively with the Word. The Digital Bible Library will provide licensees with the ability to access content from their mobile devices in a variety of formats, including audio, video, apps, websites, and print on demand.

Mart Green, the Mardel CEO mentioned in chapter 9, led the way in forming the ETEN alliance. He says, "God put the issue of Bible poverty on my heart in a significant way, and He opened many doors to make this ministry alliance a reality....The goal of Every Tribe Every Nation is to mobilize the necessary leadership and financial resources across our alliance partners so that by 2033, every tribe and every nation in the world has access to God's Word in their heart language."[3]

Computer programs are another kind of technology that has greatly accelerated the pace of Bible translation. Some of these make the linguistic analysis of a language move more quickly, some aid in the development of literacy materials, and others are directly involved in the Bible translation process.

I've already mentioned that Mandowen and Linda used a program called OurWord that allowed them to work on opposite sides of the world and sync their revisions over the Internet. Adapt It is another program that is accelerating Bible translation. You'll recall that it was designed by Bruce Waters in Papua New Guinea, who woke up one morning with the idea forming in his mind (see chapter 13).

---

3 Every Tribe Every Nation, "World's Three Major Bible Ministries Partner with Philanthropists to Create The Digital Bible Library," news release, December 13, 2012, Every Tribe Every Nation, http://www.everytribeeverynation.org/Websites/eten/files/Content/4096494/etendbllaunch-releasefinal.pdf.

Adapt It was used to produce the East Kewa New Testament in Papua New Guinea. The translation was adapted from the West Kewa New Testament with the help of Karl and Joice Franklin.

Rose Poto, a friend of Karl and Joice, was a primary school secretary whose first language was East Kewa. She also spoke West Kewa and could use that New Testament, but she knew that many in her home community could not, so she insisted that Karl help her get the Scriptures translated into East Kewa. She could not rest until her family and community had the Scriptures.

In September 2003 Karl started feeding the West Kewa translation into the Adapt It program. Rose and an East Kewa pastor worked through the computerized text word by word and phrase by phrase. Whenever they came to a word or phrase that didn't sound like East Kewa, they replaced it with the appropriate expression, and the program added that item to its memory. The next time the expression appeared in the text, the program offered them the choice of accepting the memorized expression or entering another one.

At first nearly every word or phrase had to be converted to East Kewa, and progress was slow, but as the program's memory bank filled with East Kewa words and phrases, they moved faster and faster. In less than four months, the entire first draft was done!

Like any first draft, the East Kewa translation had to be carefully checked with mother tongue speakers and consultants. Rose and her East Kewa coworkers sent many lexical and grammatical corrections to Karl, who entered them into the computer and guided the translation through typesetting and printing.

The dedication of the completed East Kewa New Testament was celebrated just twenty-two months from the day the translation was begun! Now forty thousand East Kewa speakers have access to the Scriptures.

Adapt It is also increasing the pace of translation in the Misaje language cluster project in Cameroon, where Dave and Cindy Lux and Pastor Lang work (see chapters 3 and 7). The New Testament for the Noni people (whose language is called Nooni) was dedicated in December of 2011, and the Misaje project was launched for six related languages. In just a few months a team from each of the languages, working from the Nooni New Testament and using Adapt It, produced a "pre-draft" of 30–40 percent of the New Testament in the six languages.

Remarkable progress! If they had used traditional methods, translating every verse from scratch as was necessary for the Nooni New Testament, they would have translated only 8 percent of the New Testament in that amount of time.

Similar stories could be told about the use of Adapt It for other translations around the world. Wherever there are two closely related languages, a few people who speak both languages well, and a high-quality translation in one of them, there is the potential for using Adapt It for the second translation. The program greatly reduces the amount of time needed to produce rough drafts—and thus completed translations—by building on the quality work already done on a related translation.

There is incredible power in our electronic age! God gave us airplanes, satellites, computers, sophisticated software, and the Internet to accomplish His purposes. We just have to have the eyes to see it and the imagination to use it.

THE FINISH LINE

15

UNWAVERING COMMITMENT

In 1999 Wycliffe and our international partners adopted Vision 2025—the goal of seeing a Bible translation in progress in every people group needing it by 2025. That was a bold step—a step of faith—and we all knew it came with a commitment to change the way we worked.

Dallas and I were reinvigorated by the vision and captivated by the thought of working smarter, not harder. We personally affirmed the corporate commitment to work with a renewed sense of urgency, in partnership with others, looking for creative strategies that would multiply our efforts, building capacity into others, and ensuring that what we started could be sustained.

No one knew at the time if God would honor that commitment, but He has. Since then we have been pleased to watch this commitment translated into action through cluster projects, computer adaptation, and other innovations that have delivered the Scriptures to more people faster than ever. We've watched new translation programs start at a record pace and the number of needed translation programs drop dramatically.

God is always at work behind the scenes accomplishing His purposes—and He has an unwavering commitment to His Word.

My dad is now in Heaven. I mentioned in the introduction that telling him that I would leave the family business was one of the hardest things I ever did—even though I discovered later that Dad and Mom were convinced that we were at the center of God's will for our lives. They had this faith from my birth.

I remember sitting at our kitchen table one day with a friend from Wycliffe, Alan MacDonald, who was telling Dad and me stories about a challenging part of the world where he was working. One of his responsibilities was helping translation teams get settled into new locations where they could study the local language. While he'd been successful in putting teams into several areas, there was one area and one language where he could never get permission from local officials.

One day he paid a visit to the local official responsible for granting permission to work in that area and found someone new at his desk. Thinking quickly, Alan decided to plunge right in and ask for the permission he needed. Without hesitation, the official said, "Yes, send me the paperwork and I'll sign it."

Alan was stunned. Recognizing the risk, he mustered up the courage to ask why, after so many refusals, this official was willing to grant access.

The official said, "You're American, right?" Alan acknowledged his nationality, and the official continued. "When I was a small boy, an American G.I. did me a favor—I'm returning that favor."

Looking across the table at my dad, I saw tears streaming down his face. I knew he'd spent time in that part of the world following World War II. While he never talked much about the war and fighting, he often talked about that country and the people. Years later, he still held these people in high esteem, particularly the children. Dad wondered out loud if maybe he was the one who did this man—then a boy—a favor. Maybe he was the one paying it forward. No way to know, but a very interesting and appealing thought.

After Dad died, I found a picture of him—a six-foot-three, nineteen-year-old Marine—standing head and shoulders above a group of smiling children. Dad, too, had a wide grin on his face. I still imagine small favors done in the midst of hardship that one day led to the start of a language development and translation program in a limited access country. Only God would do that.

It would be great if God would show us in advance what He has planned, but He almost never does that—at least that's my experience. Sometimes it may take years for Him to accomplish His purposes; sometimes less. Sometimes it takes a long time before we find out that He has indeed accomplished His purposes. But we can be assured He is always at work in our lives and in the circumstance in which we find ourselves. Our job is to show up, day after day, and ask Him continually what changes we need to make to live in His will for our lives.

Every three years Intervarsity's Urbana Student Missions Conference brings together students and recent graduates who are seeking God's guidance in their lives and resources to follow Him more closely. Urbana 12 took place at the end of December 2012, and though I wasn't able to attend, I followed it with great interest. One of the speakers, David Platt, challenged those in attendance to go and make disciples.

I was already familiar with David's book *Radical,*[1] in which he challenges us to rethink the American Dream, asking what we are willing to give up for the sake of the Gospel. In the book he states that this ideal—the American Dream—can work against our call to "go" as we seek to accomplish our dreams rather than God's purposes. I was also reminded of Henry Blackaby's charge to Christians in his

---

1 David Platt, *Radical: Taking Back Your Faith from the American Dream* (Colorado Springs, CO: Multnomah Books, 2010).

book *Experiencing God* (coauthored by Claude King)[2]: "Find out where God is at work and get on board!"

As David spoke, I was particularly challenged by one of the participants at Urbana who tweeted a quote, attributing it to David: "In Christ we have found someone who is worthy of losing everything for."

It struck me again: What am I willing to give up, or sacrifice, for God and His kingdom?

Probably because Urbana happened between Christmas and the New Year, the season of gift giving, this challenge started me thinking about the difference between wishing for something and actually buying it.

I am an avid online shopper. I hate shopping malls, so I'll do all I can to shop online! I do my research and then buy. While I'm doing my research, I'll often place things on a "wish list" to hold them while I look at other options.

The wish list is distinct and separate from the "shopping cart." Once I move something to the shopping cart and give my PayPal account or credit card number, I've committed myself to giving up something to obtain what I want.

So in the greater issues of life, what am I willing to move from my wish list—those things I am hoping/praying/wishing for—to my shopping cart? What am I…what are you…willing to pay for? What are we willing to sacrifice to attain what we hope for?

Even in the sacrifice, whatever that might entail, He is there asking us to trust Him in a sinful world where the inexplicable (from a human

---

2 Henry T. Blackaby, Claude V. King, and Richard Blackaby, *Experiencing God: Knowing and Doing the Will of God*, Leader Guide, revised and Expanded (Nashville, TN: LifeWay Press, 2007).

perspective) occurs. This is faith. I do not have to understand something to have faith.

Wycliffe Bible Translators and its partners are involved in the greatest acceleration of the pace of Bible translation ever witnessed! More people have more access to Scripture than ever before in the history of the Church. For the very first time there are more Bible translation programs in progress than there are Bible translation needs in the world! And it all came from that modest beginning on that mountaintop in Guatemala. Amazing!

The beginning of the final Bible translation program is within our grasp. This generation will see it happen: zero Bible translation needs; zero unreached people groups. But what will we give up to reach that goal? What will we be willing to set aside so that God can use us to accomplish His purposes?

I don't have a complete answer, nor am I willing to make anyone feel guilty about what they don't think they can set aside. That's between each of us and God. He knows I still struggle with choices like this every day. But I believe that many are being called, and that many who are called are willing to sacrifice to bring in God's kingdom. God has uniquely prepared this generation to finish the Great Commission.

THE FINISH LINE

16

THE NEW WAVE OF MISSIONS

In chapter 10 I mentioned that Dallas and I attended the graduation ceremony of twenty-three storytellers from eight different language communities in India.

They'd just completed a workshop led by Wycliffe's Elizabeth Wilson in which Bible stories were chosen that best communicated the truths of the Gospel to the target communities. With the help of skilled consultants, these mother tongue believers—all from oral cultures—learned to prepare the Bible stories to be told in oral form in their

Elizabeth Wilson

own languages, check for biblical accuracy, and test for understanding. Some of the storytellers also trained other storytellers.

The storytellers tested their stories with "story fellowship groups." In the one I observed, the storyteller told the Bible story and then encouraged discussion: "What can we learn about God from this story? How are the people in this story like people today? What can we do differently in our lives after hearing this story?"

After the stories were tested and consultant-approved, more story fellowship groups were begun. As participants listened to the stories, then repeated and discussed them, they explored new truths from God's Word using the time-tested oral methods they always used to learn new things. The stories were crafted in a way that made them easy to remember, and they spread quickly from one group to another!

Ten months after the workshop started, mother tongue Scriptures in the form of biblically accurate, culturally relevant oral stories, were available in eight languages representing sixty-five million people. In three of these languages the stories provided access to Scripture for the very first time!

The results were amazing. In an area where only 0.3 percent of the population professes to be Christian, storytellers reported that their non-Christian neighbors showed great interest in the stories. According to partners like Dr. Alexander Philip, director of the New India Evangelistic Association, the translation of stories became a church-planting effort—not only because it was an oral strategy, but also because it used the mother tongue. Using the mother tongue, he said, "just makes sense!"

Rev. Samuel Hembrom, secretary of the Brethren in Christ Church—a denomination that has worked in this region of India for seventy-five years—agreed with Dr. Philip. Rev. Hembron gave some of his personal time to help in the story project, commenting, "This is a strategic time to use the mother tongue, and we are convinced that the Lord is going to bring in a great harvest."

Following the storytelling workshop, some of the participants moved on to translating the Gospel of Luke in written form, which would become the script for the "JESUS" film—also an extremely effective tool for church planting in India.

The progression from oral stories in the mother tongue, to "JESUS" film scripts based on the Gospel of Luke, to complete New and Old Testaments supported by literacy programs—all accomplished with an abundance of partners—is proving to be an effective strategy for getting the Word into the minds and hearts of people as quickly as possible.

The abundance of partners is an essential element of this strategy. Partnerships between local language speakers (like the storytellers), national organizations (like the New India Evangelistic Association), international organizations (like Wycliffe and SIL), funding entities, and prayer supporters are a major reason the pace of Bible translation is increasing so rapidly. I am convinced that our work in the future will best be completed through partnerships.

Many of the stories I've told you demonstrate how Wycliffe and our partners are now transitioning from a primary role in Bible translation to a partnering role. One place this is especially evident is in the Americas. Cameron Townsend began our Bible translation ministry in Mexico. From there it soon spread to Peru and other parts of Latin America, and around the world.

Today only a handful of translation projects are left to start in the Americas, but the demand is growing for Old Testaments and for the revision of New Testaments that have been in use for twenty to thirty years. This demand has heavily influenced our planning for our work in the Americas. So has the fact that church and mission organizations—both indigenous and otherwise—within the various countries, are looking at the Bible translation needs around them and saying, "We can do it! In fact, we ought to do it! It should be our responsibility and our joy!"

One person who says this is Henrique Terena, president of a Brazilian organization called CONPLEI, which stands for "National Evangelical Council of Indigenous Pastors and Leaders."[1] CONPLEI is a rapidly growing organization of indigenous peoples in Brazil, and increasingly, beyond Brazil.

In 2008, under the leadership of Henrique and his vice president, Eli Ticuna, CONPLEI held a conference in Manaus that attracted twelve hundred indigenous people from forty-seven different language communities. Four years later, at their 2012 conference, they doubled their numbers—twenty-five hundred participants representing eighty-one people groups from fourteen nations.

In addition to bringing their own hammocks, musical instruments, and distinctive clothing, they brought their visions for reaching others for Christ. Most of them come from communities that just a few decades ago had not heard the Good News, nor did they have His Word available to them. Now, having claimed Christ as their own, they have gone from being recipients of the Gospel to being evangelists and missionaries in their own right.

Henrique likes to talk about three waves of missionaries in Brazil. Expatriate missionaries and Bible translators who came to the indigenous communities were the first wave. Brazilian national missionaries to the indigenous groups were the second wave. Now the third wave has begun: Brazil's indigenous people are ministering to their own people and going as missionaries to other groups. Henrique says the three waves are coming together to form a spiritual tsunami!

---

1 In Portuguese: Conselho Nacional de Pastores e Líderes Evangélicos Indígenas.

Henrique Terena, president of CONPLEI.

Part of this tsunami has to do with Bible translation. Henrique, whose mother tongue is Terena, is passionate about mother tongue translation. When he was nine years old, Wycliffe translators Nancy Butler and Muriel Ekdahl visited his village. During their weeklong stay, they told Bible stories in Terena to Henrique and his friends. Henrique was fascinated by these stories, and his heart was touched! At the end of the week, he decided to follow Jesus—all because he heard about Jesus in his own language. He went to Bible school, then became a pastor, a theological school professor, and a leader of CONPLEI.

Eli, vice president of CONPLEI, is also the product of Scripture translation. His New Testament came over the border from Peru, where it was translated for other Ticunas by Wycliffe missionaries Lambert and Doris Anderson. Eli's parents came to know the Lord through the translated Scriptures, and his father became a pastor, traveling up and down the river system teaching the Word. He often took Eli and his siblings along and made sure they read the Scriptures and prayed together every day. A Bible school graduate, Eli has also studied business administration in a Brazilian university.

With Henrique and Eli's leadership, CONPLEI has established a Bible translation program as one of its main priorities. Recognizing the value of partnerships, they have invited Wycliffe, SIL, The Seed Company, and ALEM (the Wycliffe organization in Brazil) to contribute to their translation efforts through workshops, consultant training, and funding. Most of the translators are indigenous people who gained experience by translating the New Testament with first and second wave missionaries. Now, as part of the third wave, they want to take responsibility for Old Testament translation and New Testament revision. It's their job, they say, and their joy!

As we participate in CONPLEI's tsunami, we set our sights on honoring God and spreading the vision of Bible translation for the last languages. We are committed to seeing the task through to completion. Building on Cameron Townsend's vision—which never faltered, even on his deathbed—we believe that, by God's grace, we and our partners will accomplish the task of starting and finishing the last needed Bible translation in this generation. And we remain convinced that effective evangelism and church growth rest on the foundation of the Scriptures in the mother tongue.

17

THE MISSION OF GOD AND NEW OPPORTUNITIES

I was in my first year of working in Cameroon when Emmanuel Njock walked into the office and said, "I've got it!" The piece of paper he held in his hand was the government's official recognition of The Cameroon Association for Bible Translation and Literacy—CABTAL.[1]

Emmanuel had a vision for involving Cameroonians in Bible translation, and he was convinced that what was needed was a Cameroonian organization for Cameroonians focused on finishing the remaining Bible translations needed in their country.

Twenty-five years later, in January of 2012, Dallas and I were back in Yaoundé to celebrate with our colleagues the twenty-fifth anniversary of the founding of CABTAL. It was an emotional time filled with many memories. While we in no way take credit for anything CABTAL

---

1 The vision to found CABTAL was born eight years earlier, in 1979. Cameroonian Emmanuel Njock was attending a celebration of the Lord's Supper at a church in a village in Northern Cameroon. A young man approached him and asked for help in translating the Bible into his own language. This cry for help moved Emmanuel to begin the formation of CABTAL. On October 20, 1987, the government of Cameroon officially recognized CABTAL as a non-profit association (recognized by MINAT NO 0207 of 28/10/1987 -SCIFE 5546901-)

has become, we are grateful that God used us during our eight years in Cameroon, and in subsequent years, in small ways to contribute to this historic day.

It was a milestone that represented more than just a "birthday" celebration. A picture I took during the ceremony shows Mundara Muturi, a Kenyan and the first African to serve as Africa Area director for Wycliffe Global Alliance.[2] He is honoring the outgoing general director of CABTAL, Dr. Michel Kenmogne, and the newly appointed general director, Efi Tembon. Never before has a picture like this represented so much for our organizations: Africans increasingly taking leadership roles in Bible translation across the continent.

At one point in the ceremony, the incoming director asked that everyone come forward who was on staff when CABTAL was founded in 1987, and he kept going through all the years until he reached the present day in 2012. It was really remarkable to see how many were involved, both Cameroonians and expats.

Early in its history, CABTAL's staff was dominated by people supplied by SIL, CABTAL's major partner in Cameroon. As the years progressed, however, we saw a transformation to a staff that included both expats and Cameroonians. It was not either/or but both/and: Cameroonians and expats working together to complete the task. CABTAL is today a mature, thriving organization.

CABTAL has not yet "finished" their task, but they're on their way. They have a plan and vision for starting all the remaining translation projects needed in that country, and they're now thinking about how CABTAL staff can further Bible translation beyond their geographic borders.

---

2 Wycliffe Global Alliance comprises more than forty-five member organizations and more than sixty partner organizations. The goal is that like-minded organizations worldwide can fully participate in Bible translation movements and related ministries with the benefit of shared resources, strategic relationships, and opportunities to serve together in God's mission.

Wycliffe USA, too, is contemplating what it might look like to accomplish our mission—finish the task. We're thinking not just Wycliffe USA's mission, but about the Bible translation task worldwide. We believe that having God's Word is foundational to every other mission effort, including church planting. We believe it is our contribution to the completion of the Great Commission. So how best can we do that?

We believe it still includes a very legitimate role for the expat missionary.

Since its first meeting, I have been involved with Table 71.[3] This rather unusual name was taken from "Table 71" at the Billy Graham Conference on Evangelism in Amsterdam in 2000, where a group of ministry leaders discussed strategies for reaching the remaining unreached people groups and decided to establish a working relationship. To quote the website, www.table71.org, "Table 71..." is a loose association of Christian organizations committed to working together in partnership among the remaining unreached people groups in the world in order to evangelize, make disciples, and begin and nurture indigenous church planting movements."

The association is committed to Matthew 28:18–20, where we read that Jesus commanded His disciples to go, and as they went, to make disciples of all peoples they encountered. The association is a small part of a global movement that is gaining great momentum; the goal is to finish reaching all the unreached people groups with the Good News message.

---

3 Table 71 began with a group of ministry leaders who were taking part in strategy sessions at the Billy Graham Conference on Evangelism in Amsterdam in the fall of 2000. As they strategized about how to reach unreached people groups, they asked one another what they could do to help reach all the remaining unreached people groups. In the course of their conversations, they realized that they could achieve some goals more effectively by working together more closely, and they agreed to begin working to that end immediately. There were over one hundred tables at the strategy sessions. The table where the partners had their original discussions was numbered "71," so the group began to be referred to as "Table 71."

Table 71 has defined seven essential elements in a comprehensive strategy for reaching the remaining unreached groups. One of those elements is ensuring that every people group has Scripture. The intent is to eliminate Bible poverty so that Scripture is accessible and used in the language best understood by the target audience—normally the language of birth, the mother tongue.

Steve Douglass, the president and CEO of Campus Crusade for Christ International/Cru, says it best: "Our goal for Table 71 is zero; zero unreached people groups." Reaching that goal, I believe, will require the completion of the Bible translation task. And our firm belief is that we—this generation—will finish the task.

But what does finishing look like—at least in terms of Bible translation? I think it is very different from what Cameron Townsend envisioned. When Townsend first had his vision of creating access to Scripture for every unreached people group, he thought there might be five hundred languages in the world. His goal was the New Testament for five hundred groups, and he envisioned a movement led mostly by North Americans and Europeans.

We know today that there are nearly seven thousand languages, approximately half of which have the Scripture they need. While it is still being defined, I believe our goal today might include oral stories, maybe the "JESUS" film, New Testaments, and at least parts of the Old Testament for all of these languages—completed with the involvement of literally thousands of people from hundreds of countries. It would also include ensuring that people have the skills they need to engage with the Scriptures. Zero Bible translation needs and zero unreached people groups.

It's always been in my nature to finish what I start. Even when I was a small child, my folks instilled in me that I should finish what I start. In this case, finishing is a journey toward what Paul refers to in Romans 15:20–21, "My ambition has always been to preach the Good

News where the name of Christ has never been heard, rather than where a church has already been started by someone else. I have been following the plan spoken of in the Scriptures, where it says, 'Those who have never been told about him will see, and those who have never heard of him will understand.'"

God has a plan for reaching the last people groups on earth still without His Word, still using as many people as He's called from the United States and other countries. We are all on mission with God, and He is all about finishing the task that He started. What does finishing look like? I know it includes:

- Creating true worshippers for Himself. He is the only One worthy of our worship.

- Seeing that His eternal Word is proclaimed to all people. After this, Jesus will return.

- Going to great lengths to reach just one person.

- Making sure that people from every language are represented in Heaven.

- Preserving His eternal Word for all time as a reminder of the Good News.

THE FINISH LINE

18

A CALL TO ACTION

While still working in Cameroon, I was sitting in my office in Yaoundé when a Cameroonian friend appeared. Peter Yuh was a speaker of the Kom language and was working as a teacher in the Extreme North Province of Cameroon.

Peter was troubled. He explained that his community, the Kom community, was asking him to return home to facilitate a translation of the New Testament. He was troubled because at the time he was the only college graduate in his family. That was a huge honor, but it also carried with it huge responsibilities. He told me that his family had sacrificed to send him to get an education and now he was supporting many other family members with his salary.

Peter asked for advice. Should he leave his teaching job with its dependable salary and become a Bible translator? I really didn't know what to say. Who was I to give advice to someone when I'd never experienced the responsibilities he carried? I did the only thing I could think of—I prayed with him.

Later—and I know it was after lots of thought and prayer—Peter left his "secure" teaching job, returned to his home in Belo in the Northwest Province of Cameroon, and began working with a team translating the Scriptures into Kom.

Peter Yuh at the dedication of the Kom New Testament.

Even after leaving Cameroon, I continued to follow Peter as he joined the Cameroon Association for Bible Translation and Literacy (CABTAL), went to school to get his PhD, and completed the translation project.

Dallas and I had the chance to catch up with Peter recently. He is now married, has two children, and is a translation consultant for all of West Africa.

I thought to myself, "What if Peter had said no to his community? Would they have the New Testament now? Would they have an audio recording of the New Testament? How about the "JESUS" film?" The first time it was shown, five thousand people made a commitment to follow Jesus!

But Peter said yes, and God used him to reshape his community.

More than two thousand other communities are in the process of being reshaped as well, and new projects are starting regularly. The faster the pace, the greater the need for prayer, people, and funds to sustain that pace. The adoption of Vision 2025 has exponentially increased the need for these resources. In 2008 Wycliffe Bible Translators USA launched a new effort to raise the resources we believed God was calling us to contribute toward starting, as well as finishing, Bible translations for the remaining unreached people groups on earth.

We officially launched the new effort on November 22, 2008. As I was walking to the platform to speak, I passed Zachary Peterson, the then eight-year-old son of Todd Peterson, a former player in the National Football League (NFL). Todd loves Bible translation and has contributed a significant amount of his time, talent, and resources to promote Bible translation. He and his wife, Susan, have passed this passion on to their children, Hannah and Zachary. As I passed Zachary, he jumped to his feet, reached out, and gave me an enthusiastic high five.

I still treasure the lasting image of that experience. Zachary's small act of excitement, support, and encouragement represented to me God's goodness, joy, and pleasure in that to which we were committing ourselves. It was a living, visible picture of God's enthusiasm for reaching the least, the last, and the lost.

If Vision 2025 is to be accomplished, God requires that we show up. In the midst of things that seem impossible, humanly speaking, the impossible becomes imminently possible because God sanctifies His purposes not only for our lives, but also for the nations as well.

In the Gospel of John, chapter 6, Jesus saw a crowd of at least five thousand people approaching. He asked His disciples what they should do, and they were full of human responses to a human problem. John makes it clear, however, that Jesus already knew what He was going to do. He asked the disciples to have everyone sit down. He gave thanks, broke the small amount of bread He was given, and multiplied the fish. When everyone had eaten enough, He sent His disciples to collect a huge quantity of leftovers!

All Jesus asked His disciples to do was to position the crowd—just have them sit down.

Jesus is saying the same to us today. If we have eyes to see and ears to hear, we'll recognize that something is happening in our day that no one else has seen: the number of unreached people groups—the number of Bible translation needs—is dropping rapidly. No other generation has ever seen this. This is our period of stewardship. He has asked us to show up and position ourselves to be used by Him.

And His call to us has not changed: Go, and as you go, make disciples.

On the day of Pentecost God respected the diversity of languages as a means of wonder, blessing, and communication about Himself—a way to show His power and goodness.

According to Acts 2:5–11:

At that time there were devout Jews from every nation living in Jerusalem. When they heard the loud noise, everyone came running, and they were bewildered to hear their own languages being spoken by the believers.

They were completely amazed. "How can this be?" they exclaimed. "These people are all from Galilee, and yet we hear them speaking in our own native languages....about the wonderful things God has done!"

Even then—just days after Jesus died and rose again—the Good News was being translated into other languages. Dr. Lamin Sanneh has written:

> The issue is not whether Christians translated their Scripture well or willingly, but that without translation there would be no Christianity or Christians. Translation is the church's birthmark as well as its missionary benchmark: the church would be unrecognizable or unsustainable without it. ...
>
> Whatever the language, Christians found themselves propelled toward a popular mode for translation and for communicating the message. The general rule that people had a right to understand what they were being taught was matched by the view that there was nothing God wanted to say that could not be said in simple everyday language. God would not confound people about the truth, and that made the language of religion compatible with ordinary human understanding.[1]

Just as God respects diversity of languages, so He also respects the diversity of cultures in which those languages are spoken. And yet He is not defined by those cultures. In his book *Christianity Rediscovered,* Vincent Donovan says that a missionary's greatest contribution could be to free people from their idea of God and how He works. The Gospel is outside every culture; it transcends culture, yet is destined for every culture. God must be supra-cultural or we descend into polytheism. God cannot be owned by any one culture. When God told Abraham that "all nations" would be blessed through Him, it was the beginning of the end for polytheism. God must be freed to become the high God, the God of the universe—the God referred to by Paul in Acts, chapter 17, when he describes the One the Athenians called the "Unknown God."[2]

---

1 Lamin O. Sanneh, *Whose Religion Is Christianity? The Gospel beyond the West* (Grand Rapids, MI: W.B. Eerdmans Pub., 2003), 97–98.
2 Vincent J. Donovan, *Christianity Rediscovered,* Twenty-fifth Anniversary ed. (Maryknoll, NY: Orbis Books, 2003), 34–37.

God exists in every culture long before we come, as we learn in Romans chapter 1. He has left clues about Himself within the culture—clues that we sometimes refer to as "redemptive analogies." As we build relationships within a culture, our job is to reveal this God of the universe and His Son, Jesus Christ, and this is often best done by helping people see how a story or tradition—or even a word—in their culture illustrates the message of salvation. God enables a people—any people—to reach salvation in Christ through the clues found in their cultural and tribal customs and traditions. The God of the impossible always gets there first. When God shows up, the unthinkable become unstoppable.

A proper understanding of God's Word is part of His kingdom agenda. The kingdom agenda, according to Dr. Tony Evans,[3] is "the visible manifestation and application of the comprehensive rule of God over every area of life." God's Word is transformative. It should inform and transform every aspect of life. But transformation can only take place if we can reflect on the values of the kingdom of God; if we know what God thinks; if we can understand Him because He speaks our language. God's Word is foundational!

In earlier chapters I mentioned Dave and Cindy Lux and the team they work with in the Misaje cluster (see chapters 3, 7, and 14). A translation was first completed for the Noni people (who speak the Nooni language), and then the Luxes and three of the Nooni Bible translation and literacy workers expanded their focus to include six languages related to theirs that also needed the Word.

In October 2012 Dave witnessed the first sharing of new Scripture in the six Misaje languages. He later described it in an e-mail to Paul Kimbi, a Kom language speaker and CABTAL translation consultant.

---

3 Tony Evans and his wife, Lois Evans, were awarded the Wycliffe Bible Translators USA's 2013 Scripture Impact Award for the work they have done in helping to promote Scripture translation on a global scale. Tony and Lois, who founded Oak Cliff Bible Fellowship in Dallas in 1976, have been tireless advocates for the important work of Scripture translation around the world. The Scripture Impact Award was created in 2003 in honor of the late Dr. Bill Bright, founder of Campus Crusade for Christ International (now Cru in the United States), in celebration of his love for the Lord and the Scriptures.

Dave wrote:

The Misaje translators yesterday afternoon divided up their newly printed shell books[4] of the parables of Luke for distribution. It struck me as a historic moment. It was quite unknown by the world, and equally uncared for by the world, but from God's perspective it was precious to see these men taking steps for the first time for the six language groups to have the printed Scriptures.

Paul replied:

Indeed, the world allows the more important issues of life to go unnoticed, like the entrance of the Word of God into those six communities. If it were an important government official coming into the village, the whole village would be mobilized. But here comes the Word of God (Jesus Christ), who is not to be compared to a government minister or even the president, and He comes relatively in the midst of oblivion. But God is using "the foolish things of the world to shame the wise" and "the weak things [of the world] to shame the strong" (1 Corinthians 1:27, NIV).

Significantly, on the day that the six Misaje communities received the very first bit of Scripture in their language, Dave received an e-mail from me announcing that the number of Bible translation needs in the world had dropped below two thousand for the first time in history.

Among the parables that first reached the Misaje communities were the parables of the lost sheep and the lost coin—Jesus illustrating the heart of the Father and the extent to which He will go for one person. God extending His message of grace and love to the least, the last, and the lost.

---

4 "Shell books" are booklets produced as computer files that can be printed off locally. The text can be lifted out and replaced with text in any language; the pictures and all the formatting (the "shell") remain. Shell books are often used by literacy workers as a resource for teaching adults to read and write.

I want to offer you the opportunity to be a part of this historic effort to reach the remaining people groups with the Good News of the Gospel in a language they understand best. God may be asking you to pray, to give, to go, or to advocate for Bible translation—or maybe all of the above!

You can be a part of eliminating Bible poverty and righting an injustice. You can be a part of extending the news of God's grace and love to the least, the last, and the lost. Jesus cared enough to die for them. They deserve to hear that Good News.

I invite you to visit www.wycliffe.org and see how you can become involved.

F

A FINAL WORD FROM THE AUTHOR

As I drafted this book, I would sometimes give a copy to someone for feedback. One of the early reviewers of the book said, "There sure is a lot of death involved in your writing!"

Of course if you live long enough, you have to come to grips with the reality that death is a part of life. And I honestly hadn't noticed that there was a lot of death. In fact, the last thing I want to do is leave you, the reader, with a morbid impression.

But as I reflected on what I'd written, I had to confess it was true—some of the stories are about those who were willing to make the ultimate sacrifice of their lives in order to bring in God's Kingdom here and now.

Two of my friends are now consulting in a very challenging part of the world. They were recently subjected to an armed holdup. They've been back now over that same road a few times.

John wrote, "It is a challenging environment indeed. We have been there four times within the last twelve months. On each of the four trips there was something that could easily lead us to say, 'This is enough.' We keep praying for physical protection in particular—against armed bandits and vehicle accidents...I would prefer never again to see the armed group."

Thank God, they've not said, "Enough!" My prayer for them, for each of you, and for myself is what Paul prayed for the Galatians: that no one gets fatigued and gives up doing what God has asked us to do. Because, "At the right time we will harvest a good crop if we don't give up," (Galatians 6:9–10, *The Message*).

With you on the road God called us to travel—together—toward the finish line.

Bob Creson, May 2014

A

ABOUT THE AUTHOR

Bob Creson, a native Californian, met his wife, Dallas, in high school. After marriage, college, and seven years in business, they began to feel God nudging them in a new direction. They started their journey with Wycliffe in 1983.

Geographically their "trek" has included significant stops in Paris, France; Cameroon, West Africa; Dallas, Texas; and now Orlando, Florida. Spiritually and emotionally their journey has involved an ever-growing appreciation for the transforming power of God's Word and an ever-deepening commitment to remove the barriers that prevent people from accessing and engaging with the Word.

Currently president and chief executive officer of Wycliffe Bible Translators USA, Bob has contributed to Bible translation in a variety of roles in Wycliffe Bible Translators International, SIL International (one of Wycliffe's primary partners), and The Seed Company (a Wycliffe affiliate organization). In West Africa he directed the work in Cameroon and Chad. In Texas he served as international vice president of personnel and international field director for SIL. He has served on the board of directors of SIL and currently serves on the board of the Wycliffe Global Alliance.

Bob is active on the executive committee of the Forum of Bible Agencies, North America—an association of Bible agencies and organizations that promotes the love and use of Scripture. He sits on the steering committee of Every Tribe Every Nation (ETEN), a partnership of ministries that is committed to eliminating Bible poverty, in part by maximizing the potential of digital Scriptures.

Bob attended Pepperdine University and pursued graduate studies in business management at California Lutheran College, as well as graduate studies in linguistics at the University of Oklahoma (Norman) and at the University of Texas at Arlington.

He and Dallas were married in 1973 and have four adult children: Emily (married to Paul), Scott (married to Sarah), Jeff, and Tim. They also have one grandchild, Judah.

In addition to furthering the cause of Bible translation, Bob likes eating breakfast on the lanai, reading books on missiology, hiking in the mountains with Dallas, singing Beach Boys songs with his grandson, eating kettle corn, and sharing both fun and vision on social media.